Greenland

WORLD BIBLIOGRAPHICAL SERIES

General Editors:
Robert G. Neville (Executive Editor)
John J. Horton

Robert A. Myers   Ian Wallace
Hans H. Wellisch   Ralph Lee Woodward, Jr.

John J. Horton is Deputy Librarian of the University of Bradford and currently Chairman of its Academic Board of Studies in Social Sciences. He has maintained a longstanding interest in the discipline of area studies and its associated bibliographical problems, with special reference to European Studies. In particular he has published in the field of Icelandic and of Yugoslav studies, including the two relevant volumes in the World Bibliographical Series.

Robert A. Myers is Associate Professor of Anthropology in the Division of Social Sciences and Director of Study Abroad Programs at Alfred University, Alfred, New York. He has studied post-colonial island nations of the Caribbean and has spent two years in Nigeria on a Fulbright Lectureship. His interests include international public health, historical anthropology and developing societies. In addition to *Amerindians of the Lesser Antilles: a bibliography* (1981), *A Resource Guide to Dominica, 1493–1986* (1987) and numerous articles, he has compiled the World Bibliographical Series volumes on *Dominica* (1987) and *Nigeria* (1989).

Ian Wallace is Professor of Modern Languages at Loughborough University of Technology. A graduate of Oxford in French and German, he also studied in Tübingen, Heidelberg and Lausanne before taking teaching posts at universities in the USA, Scotland and England. He specializes in East German affairs, especially literature and culture, on which he has published numerous articles and books. In 1979 he founded the journal *GDR Monitor*, which he continues to edit.

Hans H. Wellisch is Professor emeritus at the College of Library and Information Services, University of Maryland. He was President of the American Society of Indexers and was a member of the International Federation for Documentation. He is the author of numerous articles and several books on indexing and abstracting, and has published *The Conversion of Scripts* and *Indexing and Abstracting: an International Bibliography*. He also contributes frequently to *Journal of the American Society for Information Science, The Indexer* and other professional journals.

Ralph Lee Woodward, Jr. is Chairman of the Department of History at Tulane University, New Orleans, where he has been Professor of History since 1970. He is the author of *Central America, a Nation Divided*, 2nd ed. (1985), as well as several monographs and more than sixty scholarly articles on modern Latin America. He has also compiled volumes in the World Bibliographical Series on *Belize* (1980), *Nicaragua* (1983), and *El Salvador* (1988). Dr. Woodward edited the Central American section of the *Research Guide to Central America and the Caribbean* (1985) and is currently editor of the Central American history section of the *Handbook of Latin American Studies*.

VOLUME 125

Greenland

Kenneth E. Miller

Compiler

CLIO PRESS

OXFORD, ENGLAND · SANTA BARBARA, CALIFORNIA
DENVER, COLORADO

British Library Cataloguing in Publication Data

Miller, Kenneth E.
Greenland. – (World bibliographical series).
1. Greenland, history
I. Title   II. Series
016.9982

ISBN 1–85109–139–4

Clio Press Ltd.,
55 St. Thomas' Street,
Oxford OX1 1JG, England.

ABC-CLIO,
130 Cremona Drive,
Santa Barbara,
CA 93117, USA.

Designed by Bernard Crossland.
Typeset by Columns Design and Production Services, Reading, England.
Printed and bound in Great Britain by
Billing and Sons Ltd., Worcester.

THE WORLD BIBLIOGRAPHICAL SERIES

This series, which is principally designed for the English speaker, will eventually cover every country in the world, each in a separate volume comprising annotated entries on works dealing with its history, geography, economy and politics; and with its people, their culture, customs, religion and social organization. Attention will also be paid to current living conditions – housing, education, newspapers, clothing, etc.– that are all too often ignored in standard bibliographies; and to those particular aspects relevant to individual countries. Each volume seeks to achieve, by use of careful selectivity and critical assessment of the literature, an expression of the country and an appreciation of its nature and national aspirations, to guide the reader towards an understanding of its importance. The keynote of the series is to provide, in a uniform format, an interpretation of each country that will express its culture, its place in the world, and the qualities and background that make it unique. The views expressed in individual volumes, however, are not necessarily those of the publisher.

VOLUMES IN THE SERIES

For Marilyn, Susan, and Lisa,
my Scandinavian fellow travellers.

Contents

Contents

Introduction

Greenland is the world's largest island, with an area of 840,000 square miles – fifty-two times larger than Denmark, four times the size of France. The ice-free area of this vast expanse comprises only about sixteen per cent, nearly half as large as the state of Texas. The ice cap, nearly two miles thick in places, reaches the coast at many points, creating beautiful but dangerous icebergs. From the glacier at Ilulissat (Jakobshavn) an iceberg enters the ocean about every five minutes. An ice-free zone can be as wide as 120 miles but is indented with deep fjords connecting the inland ice and the ocean.

Geographically, Greenland is considered part of North America, separated from the nearest Canadian island by sixteen miles at Nares Strait. It stretches 1,660 miles from north to south and 650 miles from east to west. Its most northern point, Cape Morris Jessup, is only 460 miles from the geographic north pole, while its most southern point, Cape Farewell, is on the same latitude as Oslo. The distance between the two capes is equivalent to that between Labrador and the Gulf of Mexico. The highest point, more than 12,000 feet, is Gunnbjörns Fjeld in East Greenland.

Most of Greenland lies north of the Arctic Circle and so is subject to the extremes of the summer's midnight sun and the winter's polar darkness. The climate is Arctic, but there are wide variations. The south is affected by the masses of Arctic Ocean ice which the polar or East Greenland current brings down the eastern coast, around Cape Farewell, and up the western coast nearly to the capital Nuuk (Danish name, Godthåb). Although snow covers Greenland much of the year, many plants endure the cold conditions. There are no forests, and vegetation is mainly low grasses and heather; but even in the far north, flowers with bright blossoms flourish in the brief summer. The mildest region is the fjords on the southwestern coast. In 1986, the average temperature in Nuuk/Godthåb (which is the warmest part of Greenland) was forty-five degrees Farenheit in August, the warmest month, and fourteen degrees Farenheit in March, the coldest month. The average temperature for the year was twenty degrees.

Despite the rigours of the climate, many varieties of wildlife may be found. Animals include reindeer, caribou, musk oxen, polar bears, foxes, hares, and, starting to reappear, the Arctic wolf. Among the birds are white-tailed eagles, snow owls, ptarmigan, eider, falcons, auks, guillemots, and numerous species of gulls. In the seas are cod, Greenland halibut, Norwegian haddock, salmon, catfish, trout, scallops, shrimp, crabs, walrus, seals.

In 1988, the island's population was 54,100 with population density standing at less than 0.4 per square mile, and most of Greenland being totally uninhabited. About seventy per cent of the people live in West Greenland, in a coastal strip from Cape Farewell to Upernavik (a distance equal to that between Copenhagen and Rome). There are some 130 settlements, including airstrips and weather stations. Most are quite small. The largest town is the administrative centre, Nuuk (Godthåb) with 12,100 people.

The birthrate in 1987 was 20.1 per 1,000 population, almost twice that in Denmark. Nearly seventy-five per cent of births were out of wedlock. The abortion rate is high, 699.1 abortions per 1,000 live births in 1986, or nearly twice the Danish rate. Life expectancy figures – 60.4 years for men, 66.3 years for women – are lower than Denmark's. Much of the population is of mixed Inuit (Eskimo) and European descent. The Danish population is a stable twenty per cent of the total, but most Danes remain in Greenland for only a few years.

Native Greenlanders call their country Kalaalit Nunaat, 'the land of the Greenlanders'. Their name for themselves is Inuit, a Greenlandic word meaning 'people' (Eskimo, an Indian word, means 'meateater'). The Greenlandic language is similar to that of Inuit in Alaska and Canada, but there are major differences in dialects and no common written language. It is a polysynthetic language, that is, its words are formed as suffixes to a root so that one word can express what requires several sentences in another language. Samuel Kleinschmidt, a Moravian missionary and teacher, founded the Greenlandic written language through his translations of textbooks and the Bible.

Today, the Inuit are nearly 100 per cent literate in Greenlandic, and it has been designated the island's principal language. Danish is spoken by a large proportion of the population and is a compulsory subject in the schools. Since Danes in Greenland seldom learn Greenlandic, the working language in teaching, business, and government is often Danish. Because of the island's long association with Denmark, Greenlandic contains many Danish loan-words. Increasing numbers of young Greenlanders speak English.

The first Eskimos or Inuit to inhabit Greenland crossed the ice from the North American mainland more than 4,000 years ago. Theirs was a hunting culture, with life dependent on the supply of reindeer, polar bears, whales, walrus, and seals. Archaeological research shows at least four waves of immigration and four different Inuit cultures. Native Greenlanders today are descended from western migrants who arrived about 1000 AD.

The first European settlers arrived at nearly the same time. Erik the Red, fleeing outlawry in Iceland, landed in southern Greenland in 982 AD. He named the new territory Greenland because he thought the appellation likely to be attractive to settlers. (Erik's son, 'Leif the Lucky', sailed westward from Greenland in 1000 AD and found the place he called Vinland on the North American continent.) Other Norsemen followed Erik's path and colonized the island, establishing Osterbygden – the Eastern Settlement in the fjord district of Qaqortoq (Julianehåb) – and Vesterbygden – the Western Settlement in the fjord area behind Nuuk. The climate then was warmer than today's, and the settlers could supplement hunting and fishing with farming. By the fourteenth century, the population was 3,000-4,000. The European colonies remained for about 500 years, and then the settlers disappeared for reasons still uncertain. Worsening of the climate, failure of supplies to arrive from the mother country, bloody battles with pirates or marauding Skrellings (as they called the Inuit), have all been advanced as explanations.

At first part of the Norwegian kingdom, Greenland came under Danish rule upon the union of Denmark and Norway in 1380. After the separation of the two countries in 1814, Greenland remained Danish territory. Between 1500 and 1700, Danish monarchs tried to re-establish connections with the island but without success. The waters around Greenland were populated by Basque, English, French, Dutch, and Danish whalers, and the Dutch engaged in a little commerce with Inuit on the west coast. Traders exchanged beads, wood, iron, and textiles for furs, skins, and narwhal tusks.

But it was not until the eighteenth century that European settlements were once again established. In 1721, Hans Egede, a Danish missionary, landed near Nuuk/Godthåb, converted many Inuit to Lutheranism, and set up a chain of trading posts. A dozen years later, Moravian missionaries from Germany settled near

Egede's colony. One of the early missionaries, David Cranz, published a description of Greenland's geography, people, animals, and plants in 1765. Another missionary, Otto Fabricius, described the island's animals in the first scientific book on Greenland, *Fauna Groenlandica*, published in 1780. In 1776, after more trading sites and missionary outposts had been established, Denmark chartered the Royal Greenland Trading Company and gave it a monopoly of the Greenland trade, an arrangement that lasted until 1950. The population in 1776 had reached 5,800; a century later, it had grown to 10,000.

In 1860, Henrik Rink, a scientist and the government inspector for South Greenland, set up the first printing press and in 1861 began publishing a magazine for Greenlanders. Entitled *Atuagagdliutit* ('something for reading'), it brought Greenlanders both news from other nations and their own tales and legends. By the nineteenth century, however, most Greenlanders were poverty-stricken and many suffered from alcoholism or tuberculosis.

As a largely unknown region and a possible stopping-off point *en route* for the as yet undiscovered North West Passage to China and India, and later for the North Pole, Greenland aroused the interest of adventuresome and courageous sailors and explorers. In whaling days, William Scoresby explored and mapped the vast fjord system of Scoresby Sound. Around the middle of the last century, Greenland became the target for numerous expeditions, including the ill-fated Franklin expedition of 1845 and those of Elisha Kane in 1853 and Charles Francis Hall in 1871. The Danes largely left exploration to others until 1878 when the government created the Committee for the Direction of Geological and Geographical Research in Greenland. The Committee sent out many expeditions and published accounts of their research findings.

By the last quarter of the nineteenth century, the unmapped and unexplored inland ice attracted the attention of courageous explorers. Adolf Erik Nordenskiöld made the first serious attempt to reach the Greenland interior in 1883. In 1888, a young Norwegian, Fridtjof Nansen, with five companions made the first crossing of Greenland in the south. Robert Peary crossed the far northern ice sheet twice in the 1890s, as did the Danish explorer, Knud Rasmussen, in 1915 and 1934. Rasmussen's Thule expeditions mapped the unknown parts of northern Greenland and helped secure that region for Denmark. The twentieth century has seen many systematic efforts for scientific exploration and research in Greenland.

In the 1920s, Norway refused to recognize Danish sovereignty over northeast Greenland and claimed hunting and fishing rights there. The International Court settled the dispute in 1933 by awarding

Denmark sovereignty over all of Greenland. After Denmark's conquest by Nazi Germany in the Second World War, the Danish ambassador in Washington, Henrik Kaufman, agreed to an American military occupation of Greenland. American airbases and weather stations were set up, and American ships patrolled Greenland's waters. The local Danish administration continued in office, and its Sledge Patrol cooperated with American forces to eliminate German weather stations. At the end of the war control over Greenland reverted to Denmark, but American airfields remained at Thule and Søndre Strømfjord. These, along with various warning systems on the inland ice, continue to exist on the basis of agreements between Denmark and the United States.

In 1948 the Danish government set up a commission to consider ways of modernizing Greenland politically, economically, and socially. Its proposals brought rapid change: new investments, an import of labour from Denmark, a housing programme, expansion of the health services and a drive to wipe out tuberculosis. Political change came with the adoption in 1953 of a new constitution for Denmark, which incorporated Greenland into the realm on an equal footing with other parts of the kingdom and gave the island two members of the national parliament. Another Greenland commission in 1960 focused on economic development.

Denmark had granted Greenlanders a limited role in their local government in the 1860s by establishing appointed councils on which resident Danes and selected native Greenlanders were members. From 1911 on, local councils were popularly elected. Two regional councils also existed until their merger into one body in 1950. In the 1970s, local governments received broader powers, and in 1972, the regional council called for a study of home rule for Greenland. After several years of work, a commission with equal numbers of Danes and Greenlanders recommended autonomy, and in a referendum in January 1979, Greenland voted on home rule. The outcome was a resounding 'Yes', with a turn-out of sixty-three per cent of the electorate, 12,754 voters (seventy-three per cent) were for home rule, 4,705 against it.

The Danish parliament approved a Home Rule Act which went into effect on 1 May 1979. The Act transferred most powers over internal affairs to a new Greenland government but left constitutional matters, foreign relations, defence, and national finance in the hands of the Danish government. The national and Greenland governments have joint authority over Greenland's oil and mineral resources.

Under home rule Greenland has its own legislature, the Landsting, and its own executive, the Landsstyre or home rule government. The Landsting's single house has a minimum of twenty-three members, elected by proportional representation in eight constituencies. Four more members may be added to the body to ensure a fair representation of the votes cast. Elections take place every four years unless the Landsting is dissolved earlier. Danish citizens who are at least eighteen years old and resident in Greenland for at least six months prior to an election have the right to vote. Members of the Landsting are native Greenlanders since Danes, whose residence in the island is usually brief, are not politically active.

A premier or 'home government head' leads the executive, supported by four or five ministers. The executive is responsible to the Landsting. The Greenland government maintains an office in Copenhagen, and Denmark is represented by a high commissioner in Godthåb/Nuuk.

The court system is like that of Denmark and consists of eight circuit courts and a high court. A circuit court, staffed by a lay magistrate and two lay associates, hears civil and criminal cases in its area. The high court, with a judge and two lay justices, hears appeals. Cases may be appealed from the high court to the Supreme Court of Denmark. Greenland has its own criminal code, unique in its stress on education and rehabilitation rather than imprisonment, a concept alien to the Greenlandic sense of justice. Offenders may serve sentences in open correctional institutes, working outside them during the day, but a person convicted of a serious crime like murder or rape may be sent to Denmark for confinement in a prison.

Four political parties compete for seats in the Landsting. Atassut (Solidarity) favours close ties with Denmark and opposed leaving the European Community. Siumut (Forward) wants the greatest possible autonomy for Greenland within the union of Denmark, Greenland and the Faroe Islands, and is affiliated with the Danish Social Democratic party. Inuit Ataqatigiit (Human Brotherhood) is politically farther to the left, advocates independence, and strongly favoured Greenland's withdrawal from the European Community. The newest and smallest party, Issittup-Partiia (Polar Party) calls for more privatization of the economy. In the May 1987 elections to the Landsting, Atassut and Siumut each won eleven seats; Inuit Ataqatigiit captured four and Issitup-Partiia one. Siumut has been in office since 1979, in coalition with Inuit Ataqatigiit since 1984. In 1990, the home government head (premier) was Jonathan Motzfeldt of Siumut.

Greenland's economy depends heavily on fishing – nearly a third of the population depend on it directly or indirectly. About ten per cent of the people still make their living from hunting and sealing. A small number are engaged in sheep-farming. Handicrafts of bone, stone, leather, beads, and wood supplement the incomes of some families.

Greenland has deposits of iron, uranium, copper, coal, cryolite, silver, lead, and zinc, but only the last four are currently mined, and production is small. The search for oil has been disappointing, but there are prospects in eastern Greenland and on the continental shelf in the southeast although the cost of extraction would be very high.

The Greenland government took over the Royal Greenland Trading Company in 1985 and renamed it Kallalit Niuerfiat (KNI). KNI has some fifty-four production plants whose 2,500 employees process prawn, halibut, cod, redfish, salmon, catfish, and lamb. In 1986, fishing, sealing, and agricultural products made up eighty-two per cent of Greenland's exports, and lead, zinc, and chrome ore fourteen per cent. Principal customers are Denmark, France, Germany, the United States, and Finland. About seventy-five per cent of Greenland's imports – consumer goods and materials needed for business and industry – come from, or via, Denmark.

The paucity of developed resources and the heavy reliance on the fishing industry present problems for Greenlanders and their standard of living. Much depends on the forces of nature. A slight change in climate in the mid-1960s, for example, lowered the seawater temperature and drastically reduced the cod catch. In 1977, Greenland imposed a 200-nautical mile fishing zone, and its government enforces quotas on catches for major species of fish and promotes conservation measures. Economic development in the post-Second World War years brought with it increased social disorganization and has not eliminated poverty. Unemployment is very high among young people. The suicide rate has climbed and alcoholism is a problem. In 1988, Greenlanders over the age of fifteen consumed on average the equivalent of seventeen litres of 100 per cent alcohol each (comparable figures for Denmark and Sweden were 11.8 and 6.4) and this represented a decline in consumption from the early years of the 1980s! It has been estimated that nine out of every ten crimes committed in Greenland are alcohol-related. Denmark's national treasury continues to provide a substantial annual subsidy to Greenland, and this, along with revenues from local taxes, goes mainly to support health services and education. The general standard of health among the population has been raised considerably since the 1950s.

Despite Greenland's small population, the island has a great deal of cultural activity. Det Grønlandske Forlag (the Greenland Publishing Company) issues as many as fifty titles in Greenlandic each year, some of which are new titles and others which are translations. Most are printed by Sydgrønlands Bogtrykkerie (South Greenland Book Printers), a firm that has been active for more than a century. The art school at Godthåb/Nuuk attracts students from all over the country.

Introduction

There are local libraries, a national library, and a national museum. Tukaq, a professional theatre company, gives performances, primarily in Greenlandic, in schools and meeting halls and a few towns have amateur dramatic societies. Sports flourish; more than 100 clubs with 20,000 active members, are joined together in the Greenland Sports Federation, with associations for soccer and skiing having the largest memberships.

As far as the mass media is concerned, Radio Greenland broadcasts both radio (with programmes mainly in Greenlandic) and television (which offers much the same fare as Danish TV although presenting some Greenlandic and dual-language programmes). There are two Greenlandic–Danish dual-language weekly newspapers, several trade journals, and a number of small local papers. Education is compulsory for nine years, and most students go on to complete up to four years more with those who want a higher education generally attending a Danish university. The Church of Greenland is part of Denmark's established Evangelical Church, and there is also a Catholic Church in the capital.

When Denmark voted in 1973 to join the European Community, Greenland also became part of the EC, even though sixty-nine per cent of its voters had rejected membership. Many Greenlanders believed that the EC ignored their interests and thought that EC policies hampered the island's economic development. In February 1982, they voted in a referendum to leave the EC – the margin was narrow: 12,624 (fifty-three per cent) in favour, and 11,174 against. Several years of negotiation produced an agreement with the EC, under which the Community provides compensation for continued access to Greenland waters by its members' fishing fleets and Greenlanders have retained the right to sell their catch in EC countries without tariff restrictions. Greenland officially terminated its EC membership on 1 February 1985, but remains affiliated with the Community in the same way that many former European colonies are.

Greenland sends its own delegation to the Nordic Council, a regional body that promotes cooperation among Denmark, Finland, Iceland, Norway and Sweden. It is also a member of the Inuit Circumpolar Conference (ICC) which brings Greenlanders together with the Inuit of Alaska and Canada and the chief concerns of which are the furthering of cultural relations and protection of the Arctic environment.

The bibliography
Each volume in the World Bibliographical Series seeks to provide a selective, annotated bibliography, covering all aspects of a particular

country, for an audience that includes both the general reader and the specialist.

In accordance with the Series' objectives, therefore, I have presented a wide range of material, giving preference to recently published works but including older ones when they remain among the best sources of information on their topics, or when they are of historical interest. I have also included a number of recent periodical articles.

Within the bibliography, citations within a section have been arranged alphabetically by author or compiler, or, in their absence, by title.

The reader who desires additional information on a topic is advised to write to Greenland Home Government (Grønlands Hjemmestyre), Postbox 1015, DK-3900 Nuuk/Godthåb, Greenland, or Greenland Home Government – Denmark Bureau (Grønlands Hjemmestyres Danmarkskontor), Sjæleboderne 2, DK-1122, Copenhagen K, Denmark. Some publications of the Greenland government are available in English.

Without the aid of a number of people, the work of compiling this bibliography would have been much more difficult, and I am grateful to those who helped: Gioia Lucente, my research assistant; the librarians at Dana Library, Rutgers University, Newark, New Jersey (and especially Wanda Gawienowski), who pursued inter- and intra-library loan materials; and my wife Marilyn, who provided encouragement and helpful criticism. Errors are my responsibility, not theirs.

Greenland and its People

1 **The national park in north-east Greenland.**
Gregers E. Andersen, Claus Andreasen, Henning Brøndsted, Bent
Fredskild, Martin Ghisler, Frede Madsen, Christian Vibe.
Godthåb/Nuuk: Forskning/tusaut, Commission for Scientific Research in
Greenland, 1984. 32p. maps.
A huge uninhabited area of northeastern Greenland is the world's largest national
park. In this special English version of a newsletter published by the Commission for
Scientific Research in Greenland, researchers connected with the Commission and the
National Park Board discuss the park's history, administration, botanical studies,
historical artifacts, animals, geodetic research, and geology and mineral resources.

2 **Greenland.**
Michael Banks.   Newton Abbott, England: David & Charles, 1975.
208p. maps. bibliog.
A description of the exploration, geography, history, and wildlife of Greenland. The
author, a climber as well as an explorer, discusses his experiences in mapping the
Greenland ice fields and his travels throughout the island.

3 **Facts about Denmark.**
Mette Koefoed Bjørnson, Erik Hansen, translated from the Danish by
Erik Langkjær.   Copenhagen: Politiken, 1976. 19th ed. 104p. maps.
A small book for the general reader, crammed with basic facts on most aspects of life
in Denmark, Greenland, and the Faroe Islands. Subjects covered include population,
living standards, marriage and divorce, sports, religion, education, culture, economy,
money and banking, government and administration, defence and foreign policy.
Revised editions are published at frequent intervals.

1

4 **The Arctic.**
Fred Bruemmer.   New York: New York Times Book Company, in
cooperation with the *Montreal Star*, 1974. 224p. maps. bibliog.
Many photographs from Greenland and other Arctic regions, both in colour and black-
and-white, are incorporated in this volume, along with brief commentaries on
exploration, geography, plants, animals, and people.

5 **Greenland.**
Edited by Kristjan Bure, translated from the Danish by Reginald Spink,
A. Anslev.   Ringkjøbing, Denmark: A. Rasmussen, for the Royal
Danish Ministry of Foreign Affairs, 1961. 192p. map.
A collection of articles by Danish authors on Greenland's geography, administration,
history, culture, daily life, industries and occupations, and scientific exploration.
Included are many interesting photographs of people, life, and landscapes.

6 **Two summers in Greenland: an artist's adventures among ice and islands,
in fjords and mountains.**
A. Riis Carstensen.   London: Chapman & Hall, 1890. 185p. map.
An artist's chronicle of his adventures in Greenland ('this glorious land', as he called
it) and his observations of the Greenlanders in the summers of 1884 and 1888.

7 **Crown of the world: a review of the inner Arctic.**
Cora Cheney, Ben Partridge.   New York: Dodd, Mead, 1979. 223p.
bibliog.
A general introduction to the Arctic lands, based on eighteen months of travel by the
authors through Greenland and other parts of the region. They present their views on
the problems facing the people and animals of the Arctic and on the difficulties of
preserving a fragile ecological balance.

8 **Handbook of North American Indians. Volume 5. Arctic.**
Edited by David Damas.   Washington, DC: Smithsonian Institution,
1984. 829p. map. bibliog.
A very complete compendium of information on the Arctic peoples. Besides general
discussions of archaeology, ethnology, the physical environment and ecosystems,
languages, and prehistory, a section on Greenland (p. 522-645, 700-28) has
contributions from authorities on the island's prehistory and history, palaeo-Eskimo
cultures, the polar Eskimo. written literature, contemporary Greenland, and the pan-
Eskimo movement. The bibliography is extensive, and there are many illustrations.

9 **Denmark: an official handbook, 1974.**
Copenhagen: Press and Cultural Relations Department, Royal Danish
Ministry of Foreign Affairs, 1974. 902p. maps. bibliog.
The indispensable starting point for facts about Denmark, this volume provides concise
and accurate information about virtually every aspect of the Danish past and present.
Greenland is included in every appropriate section. The selections are contributed by
leading Danish scholars or participants in the activity described, and the book is well
illustrated with a lengthy bibliography.

2

10 **Greenland: then and now.**
Erik Erngaard, translated from the Danish by Mona Giersing.
Copenhagen: Lademann, 1972. 240p. maps. bibliog.
An anecdotal survey that affords a good introduction to Greenland from prehistoric
times to the 1970s. There is much information on most aspects of the island's history
and the life of its people over the centuries, accompanied by a great many black-and-
white and colour illustrations.

11 **North, Central and South America: Atlantic Islands.**
Foreign Office, Great Britain, Historical Section. London: HM
Stationery Office, 1920. (Peace Handbooks, volume XXI, no. 132). 37p.
bibliog.
This section of a series of studies prepared by the Foreign Office for British delegates
to the Versailles peace conference summarizes information about Greenland at the end
of the First World War: geography, population, history, social, political, and economic
conditions, industry and commerce, natural resources, fisheries.

12 **Some characteristic problems in present-day Greenland.**
Borge Fristrup. In: *The Arctic circle: aspects of the north from the
circumpolar nations.* Edited by William C. Wonders. Don Mills,
Ontario: Longmans Canada, 1976, p. 63-85. map. bibliog.
More a general survey of Greenland's history, population, and economic development
than an analysis of its problems.

13 **Greenland.**
Copenhagen: Press and Cultural Relations Department, Royal Danish
Ministry of Foreign Affairs, 1987. 23p. map. (Facts About Denmark).
A brief survey of Greenland, in English.

14 **Greenland: past and present.**
Edited by Knud Hertling, Erik Hesselbjerg, Svend Klitgaard, Ebbe
Munck, Olaf Petersen. Copenhagen: Edvard Henriksen, [1968.] 370p.
An authoritative survey of most aspects of Greenland. Specialists contribute thirty
articles covering geography and geology, flora and fauna, history, language, political,
social, and economic development, law, religion, education, art and poetry, press and
radio. Many black-and-white photos complement the text.

15 **Arctic Riviera: a book about the beauty of north-east Greenland.**
Ernst Hofer. Bern, Switzerland: Kümmerly & Frey, 1957. 125p.
A professional photographer narrates his experiences in four expeditions to Greenland
and illustrates his words with photographs of the scenery and the plant and animal life.

16 **Greenland: a part of Denmark.**
Tom Høyem. In: *There is something wonderful in the State of Denmark*. Edited by Arne Melchior, translated by Esther Aagaard Tapelband. Secaucus, New Jersey: Lyle Stuart, 1987, p. 124–33.

A former cabinet minister for Greenland discusses the island's strategic importance, reforms and the introduction of Home Rule, Arctic research, and economic change.

17 **Arctic dreams: imagination and desire in a northern landscape.**
Barry Lopez. New York: Charles Scribner's Sons, 1986. 464p. maps. bibliog.

Both a celebration of the Arctic landscape and the people and animals that live there and a book about the dreams that have drawn people to the Arctic. Although Greenland is touched on only briefly, much of the island's life can be perceived in the larger context.

18 **Leaves from a Greenland diary.**
Ruth Bryan Owen. New York: Dodd, Mead, 1935. 166p.

A tourist's-eye view of Greenland in the 1930s, as reported in a day-to-day journal of a brief visit by the then American ambassador to Denmark.

19 **The polar regions: an anthology of Arctic and Antarctic photographs.**
Edited by J. M. Scott. New York: Oxford University Press; London: Chatto & Windus, [n.d.]. 100p.

The book is almost entirely a collection of black-and-white photographs, including many from Greenland: Johnstrup Mountain in East Greenland, glaciers, Arctic animals, Eskimos, dog sledges, umiaks and kayaks, a cryolite mine. The author provides a brief introduction.

20 **The Viking circle: Denmark, Greenland, Norway, Sweden, Finland, Iceland.**
Colin Simpson. New York: Fielding Publications in association with William Morrow, 1968. 366p. maps.

Information for the traveller to Scandinavia, with personal observations drawn from the author's experience. Included is a section on Greenland (p. 295-348).

21 **Ship in the wilderness.**
J. Snyder, Keith Shackleton. London: Dent, 1986. 208p.

The MS *Lindblad Explorer* has carried tourists to many regions of the world, including Greenland. Its voyages are chronicled in this book, along with a number of paintings by Keith Shackleton.

22 **Within the circle: portrait of the Arctic.**
Evelyn Stefansson.   New York: Charles Scribner's Sons, 1945. 160p.
maps.

A popularly written introduction to the Arctic by the wife of the noted explorer. The chapter on Greenland (p. 9-15) gives a brief summary emphasizing Denmark's desire to keep Greenland closed from the world but noting that this will have to change when the war ends.

23 **Greenland.**
Edited by M. Vahl, G. C. Andrup, L. Bobé, Ad. S. Jensen.
Copenhagen: C. A. Reitzel; Oxford: Humphrey Milford, Oxford
University Press, 1928-29. 3 vols. maps.

A compendium of virtually everything that was known about Greenland as of the 1920s. The coverage is comprehensive, with chapters written by experts. Volume one examines cartography, geography, flora and fauna, physiography. Volume two discusses present-day Greenlanders, their intellectual culture, and archaeology. Volume three covers the island's status in international law, a history of trade and colonization, the Church of Greenland, missionary activities, education, health, and mining.

24 **Greenland.**
Lars Vesterbirk.   Copenhagen: Royal Danish Ministry of Foreign
Affairs, 1983. 12p. map. (Factsheet Denmark).

A brief introduction to Greenland's geography, history, constitutional status, government, political parties, economy, education, cultural activities, and foreign relations.

Iceland and Greenland.
See item no. 343.

Explorations

General

25 **From the ends of the earth: an anthology of polar writings.**
Edited by Augustine Courtauld. London: Oxford University Press,
1958. 423p. map. bibliog.
This collection includes an extract from the Icelandic Saga of Erik the Red, telling of
the discovery and settlement of Greenland, as well as selections from the narratives of
such Greenland explorers as Martin Frobisher, John Davis, William Baffin, Hans
Egede, David Krantz, Hans Saabye, Vilhelm Graah, and Vilhjalmur Stefansson.

26 **The discoverers: an encyclopedia of explorers and exploration.**
Edited by Helen Delpar. New York: McGraw-Hill, 1980. 471p. maps.
bibliog.
Contains concise biographies of pre-eminent explorers, including a number related to
Greenland: Leif Ericksson, Adolf Nordenskiöld, Fridtjof Nansen, Robert Peary,
Vilhjalmar Stefansson. An article on Greenland summarizes the history of its
explorations, and another discusses Norse maritime discoveries, including voyages to
Greenland.

27 **The Greenland ice cap.**
Børge Fristrup, translated from the Danish by David Stoner.
Copenhagen: Rhodos; Seattle, Washington: University of Washington
Press, 1967. 312p. maps. bibliog.
This volume, by a Danish scientist and explorer who has led important expeditions to
Greenland, gives a history of the discovery and exploration of the Greenland ice cap
and explains how scientific research is gradually revealing its mysteries. Covering the
period from Erik the Red to the present, the author draws not only upon his first-hand
experiences but also upon ancient and contemporary documents and scientific studies.

The book is beautifully illustrated with photographs (many in colour) by Fristrup, along with photographs from the collections of other expeditions.

28 **A history of polar exploration.**
L. P. Kirwan.   New York: W. W. Norton, 1960. 374p. maps. bibliog.
A former director of the Royal Geographic Society succinctly relates the story of Arctic and Antarctic exploration. The account, which was published in England as *The white road* (London: Hollis & Carter, 1959), includes discussions of the many voyages to Greenland and the Greenland waters. Among the expeditions chronicled are those of Erik the Red (10th century), Martin Frobisher (1576), Elisha Kent Kane (1853-55), Fridtjof Nansen (1888–89), Robert Peary (1892, 1895), and Knud Rasmussen (1912). A paperback edition was later published with the title *History of polar exploration* (Harmondsworth, England: Penguin, 1962).

29 **The scientific exploration of Greenland from the Norsemen to the present.**
Fritz Loewe.   Columbus, Ohio: Ohio State University, 1970. 19p. map. bibliog. (Institute of Polar Studies Report No. 35).
Discusses the reasons for the exploration of Greenland and summarizes the principal scientific expeditions from the eighteenth century to the 1960s. The author concludes that Greenland will be 'a favored field of scientific exploration for a long time'.

30 **The lands of silence: a history of Arctic and Antarctic exploration.**
Sir Clements R. Markham.   Cambridge, England: Cambridge University Press, 1921. 539p. maps. bibliog.
A history of virtually all the explorations of the Arctic and Antarctic regions from the Vikings to the early twentieth century. The volume includes the Greenland voyages sponsored by Christian IV in the early 1600s, the missionary expeditions of Hans Egede, and explorations of Greenland's east coast and the inland ice.

31 **Safe return doubtful: the heroic age of polar exploration.**
John Maxtone-Graham.   New York: Charles Scribner's Sons, 1988. 364p. maps. bibliog.
A very readable chronicle of polar explorations, including the expeditions to Greenland by Adolphus Greely, Charles Francis Hall, Elisha Kent Kane, Fridtjof Nansen, and Robert Peary.

32 **To the Arctic! The story of northern exploration from earliest times to the present.**
Jeannette Mirsky.   New York: A. A. Knopf, 1948. 334p. maps. bibliog.
This revised version of the author's *To the north* (published in 1934) is a history of northern explorations from the earliest recorded voyages to 1932, intended for the general reader. A lengthy chapter on Greenland discusses Hans Egede and the beginnings of modern Greenland and the explorations of the east coast and the inland ice cap by such men as Peary, Nansen, and Nordenskiöld.

33 **A history of polar exploration.**
David Mountfield.   London: Book Club Associates, and New York:
Dial Press, 1974. 208p. bibliog.
A readable and well-illustrated history of Arctic and Antarctic explorations, including
a brief examination of the discovery and early settlement of Greenland, as well as
exploits of later explorers.

34 **Eskimos and explorers.**
Wendell H. Oswalt.   Novato, California: Chandler & Sharp, 1970.
349p. maps. bibliog.
This traces the emergence of Eskimos from the time that Europeans thought them
more legendary than real, through the first European encounters with them in
Greenland about AD 1000, to the last explorations of their lands. Discussed are the
early Viking settlements in Greenland, the renewal of contacts by the Danes in the
seventeenth century and the work of Hans Egede in the eighteenth century, and the
contrasting Eskimo ways of life in West Greenland and East Greenland.

35 **The private life of polar exploration.**
J. M. Scott.   Edinburgh: William Blackwood, 1982. 177p. maps.
An Arctic explorer's account of the dangers and adventures of Arctic exploration.
Among the tales are the stories of the mysterious death of Charles Francis Hall in
Greenland in 1871 and the loss of Dr. Alfred Wegener on the Greenland ice sheet in
1930. The dispute over the cause of Hall's death – an acute digestive disorder or
murder by arsenic – has never been resolved. Wegener and a companion died from
exhaustion and exposure on a winter journey from their remote weather station to the
coast.

Greenland.
See item no. 2.

The Arctic.
See item no. 4.

Greenland.
See item no. 5.

The fiord region of East Greenland.
See item no. 98.

**The polar regions: a physical and economic geography of the Arctic and
Antarctic.**
See item no. 99.

The Nordic seas.
See item no. 103.

Greenland.
See item no. 180.

Arctic exploration.
See item no. 340.

Early voyages

36 The Norse discoveries of America: the Wineland sagas.
G. M. Gathorne-Hardy.   Oxford: Clarendon, 1970. 304p. maps.
bibliog.
This is comprised of translations by the author of documents and sagas relating to Vinland (the Norse settlements in North America), along with his commentaries on them. Of special reference to Greenland are 'Eric the Red and the colonization of Greenland', 'The adventure of Bjarni Herjulfson', 'Gudrid comes to Greenland', and 'Gudrid and the sybil',

37 The Norse Atlantic saga, being the Norse voyages of discovery and settlement to Iceland, Greenland and America.
Gwyn Jones.   London: Oxford University Press, 1986. 2nd ed. 337p.
maps. bibliog.
An account of the Norse voyages of discovery and exploration to Iceland, Greenland and the east coast of North America and their efforts to colonize all three areas. Included are translations of sources, including 'The Greenlanders' saga' (late twelfth or early thirteenth century) and 'Erik the Red's saga' (circa 1263).

38 A history of the Vikings.
T. D. Kendrick.   New York: Barnes & Noble, 1968. 412p. maps.
bibliog.
Kendrick covers both the history of the Viking homelands in Scandinavia and their travels to Russia, Western Europe, the British Isles, the Faroes, Iceland, Greenland, and America. The author discusses the discovery of Greenland by Erik the Red and the first settlements in the tenth century, the introduction of Christianity in 1000 AD, the decline and disappearance of the colony in the fifteenth century, and archaeological findings about the early Norse settlers.

39 Herdsmen & hermits: Celtic seafarers in the northern seas.
T. C. Lethbridge.   Cambridge: Bowes & Bowes, 1950. 146p. maps.
bibliog.
Several chapters of this volume consider the discovery and settlement of Greenland and the life of the early Norsemen there.

40 Vikings!
Magnus Magnusson.   New York: E. P. Dutton, 1980. 320p. bibliog.
A history of the Viking Age and a discussion of its myths and realities. It begins with the mythological, literary, and historical contexts and proceeds to separate examinations of the Vikings of Denmark, Norway, and Sweden. The sections on Denmark describe the Vikings from their first assaults on Western Europe to the reign of Harald Blue-Tooth, and discuss the Danish invasions of England, the colonization of Greenland, and the Anglo-Viking empire of King Canute. The author's practical knowledge of archaeology makes him an excellent guide to the sites and treasures of the Viking world. The book is richly illustrated with colour and black-and-white photographs.

41 **Viking expansion westwards.**
Magnus Magnusson. London: Bodley Head; New York: Henry Z.
Walck, 1973. 152p. maps. bibliog.
A chronicle of the Viking expansion to the west from the ninth to the twelfth centuries, and a discussion of everyday life and traditions in Viking settlements as revealed by archaeological discoveries. A chapter on Greenland provides a history of its discovery and settlement and a description of life in its early farming communities.

42 **The Vinland sagas: the Norse discovery of America. Grænlendinga saga and Eirik's saga.**
Translated by Magnus Magnusson and Hermann Pálsson. New York:
New York University Press, 1966; Harmondsworth, England: Penguin,
1968. 124p. maps.
These medieval Icelandic sagas tell the tales of Erik the Red's colonization of Greenland and of his son Leif's voyage to the New World. The translators contribute an extensive introduction.

43 **The conquest of the North Atlantic.**
G. J. Marcus. Woodbridge, England: Boydell & Brewer, 1980; New
York: Oxford University Press, 1981. 224p. maps. bibliog.
Included in this discussion of early voyages to the North Atlantic are the Viking discovery and settlement of Greenland and the last ventures there in the early fifteenth century.

44 **The European discovery of America. Volume 1: The northern voyages AD 500-1600.**
Samuel Eliot Morison. New York: Oxford University Press, 1971.
712p. maps. bibliog.
This informally written but authoritative history by the noted naval historian tells of early European voyages to North America, including events relating to Greenland: its discovery by Norsemen about AD 985, its early settlements, the disappearance of European settlers, and its later rediscovery and exploration.

45 **In northern mists: Arctic exploration in early times.**
Fridtjof Nansen, translated from the Norwegian by Arthur G. Chater.
New York: Frederick A. Stokes, 1911. 2 vols. maps. bibliog.
A description by the famous Norwegian explorer of voyages of exploration to the Arctic, from the fabled journeys of antiquity to the expeditions of the Portuguese and John Cabot in the sixteenth century. Included are detailed accounts of the Viking discovery of Greenland, its settlement in the tenth century, Viking explorations of its east and west coasts, the origins of the 'skrellings' or Eskimos and their relationships with the European immigrants, and the decline and disappearance of the European settlements by the early fifteenth century.

46 **Northern mists.**
Carl O. Sauer.   Berkeley and Los Angeles, California: University of California Press; London: Cambridge University Press, 1968. 204p. maps.

A history of explorations westward from Europe in the Middle Ages. Chapter six (p. 100-39) describes the discovery of Greenland in the tenth century, its settlement by Erik the Red, and voyages to Vinland. Chapter seven (p. 140-57) speculates on reasons for the failure of the Norse colony in Greenland after 500 years.

47 **Ultima Thule.**
Vilhjalmur Stefansson.   New York: Macmillan, 1940. 383p. maps. bibliog.

Examines what is known about early explorers who may or may not have reached Greenland and other Arctic regions before the Vikings. The author scrutinizes writings attributed to Pytheas, Columbus and others and compares their accounts with the findings of modern explorers.

48 **The heroic age of Scandinavia.**
G. Turville-Petre.   London, New York: Hutchinson's University Library, 1951. 196p. bibliog.

Discusses literary and archaeological sources, legendary and real heroes, Viking civilization in Denmark and Norway, and the explorations and incursions of the Vikings in Greenland and other areas in the years before AD 1030.

49 **The Vikings and their origins: Scandinavia in the first millennium.**
David M. Wilson.   New York: McGraw-Hill, 1970. 144p. maps. bibliog.

The history, culture, and warfare of the Vikings from the beginning of the Christian era to about AD 1100, including a brief summary of their discovery and early settlement of Greenland.

The discoverers: an encyclopedia of explorers and exploration.
See item no. 26.

17th, 18th, and 19th centuries

50 **Doctor Kane of the Arctic seas.**
George W. Corner.   Philadelphia: Temple University Press, 1972. 306p. maps.

A biography of the Arctic explorer (1820-57), drawing on the Kane family papers and other primary sources. Kane made important contributions to Arctic geography, including his mapping of the waterway between western Greenland and Ellesmere

Island and his discovery of the Humboldt Glacier which spills over from the Greenland ice cap.

51   **Danish Arctic expeditions, 1605 to 1620. Book I, the Danish expeditions to Greenland in 1605, 1606, and 1607, to which is added Captain James Hall's voyage to Greenland in 1612.**
      Edited by C. C. A. Gosch.   New York: Burt Franklin, [n.d.]. 205p. maps.

The reports of four voyages of exploration to Greenland in the early seventeenth century. Three of the accounts are written by James Hall, chief pilot for three of the expeditions and captain of the fourth. This work was originally published by the Hakluyt Society (London, 1897).

52   **Three years of Arctic service: an account of the Lady Franklin Bay Expedition of 1881-84 and the attainment of farthest north.**
      Adolphus W. Greely.   London: Richard Bentley; New York: Charles Scribner's Sons, 1886. 2 vols. maps.

The official account of an American expedition to the Arctic during the First International Polar Year, 1882-83. It includes descriptions of two journeys to the north coast of Greenland and a brief summary of the knowledge about Greenland and its people in the 1880s.

53   **An Arctic boat journey, in the autumn of 1854.**
      Isaac I. Hayes.   Boston, Massachusetts: Brown, Taggard, & Chase; Philadelphia: J. B. Lippincott; New York, Sheldon, 1860. 375p. maps.

The surgeon of the second Grinnell expedition relates the story of the unsuccessful, four-month effort by a small party of explorers to reach Upernavik in northern Greenland. The book emphasizes the rigours and miseries of travel – the storms, dangerous seas and ice floes, and difficulties with the Eskimo – but concludes that the perils encountered by Arctic travellers are generally less than those met by travellers in Africa.

54   **The land of desolation; being a personal narrative of observation and adventure in Greenland.**
      Isaac I. Hayes.   New York: Harper & Brothers, 1872. 357p.

A description of a visit to the coasts of Greenland in the summer of 1869 by a party more interested in scenery (for the artist William Bradford) than in science. The book describes icebergs, glaciers, and the ruins of Viking colonies and has some observations on the life of Greenlanders and the government of the island by Denmark.

55   **The open polar sea: a narrative of a voyage of discovery towards the north pole in the schooner 'United States'.**
      Isaac I. Hayes.   New York: Hurd & Houghton, 1867. 454p. maps.

An account by its leader of an 1860 expedition of exploration to the Arctic that included a survey of the northern coast of Greenland. Hayes's objective was discovery of a sea passage from the Atlantic to the Pacific across the North Pole; but, failing in this, his principal accomplishment was a slight extension of knowledge about the region around Ellesmere Island.

56 **North-east passage: Adolf Erik Nordenskiöld, his life and times.**
George Kish. Amsterdam: Nico Israel, 1973. 283p.
A biography of the noted nineteenth century explorer, with a full account of his journeys to Greenland from the first expedition in 1870 to the last in 1883. The work is based on the Nordenskiöld papers in the library of the Royal Swedish Academy of Sciences.

57 **The Arctic voyages of Adolf Eric Nördenskiöld, 1858-1879.**
Alexander Leslie. London: Macmillan, 1879. 447p. maps. bibliog.
Describes the expeditions of the Arctic explorer, including his arduous trip across the Greenland ice in 1870.

58 **Narrative of discovery and adventure in the polar seas and regions: with illustrations of their climate, geology, and natural history; and an account of the whale-fishery.**
John Leslie, Robert Jameson, Hugh Murray. New York: J. & J. Harper, 1833. 373p. map.
An example of how Greenland and other Arctic regions were presented to the general but serious reader in the early nineteenth century. Topics considered include climate, flora and fauna, voyages of exploration, geology, and whale-fishing. The authors comment that 'the scenery is awful and dreary, yet abounds in striking, sublime, and even beautiful objects'.

59 **The voyages of William Baffin, 1612-1622.**
Edited by Sir Clements Robert Markham. New York: Burt Franklin, [n.d.]. maps.
Contains Baffin's descriptions of Greenland from his journal of the voyage of 1612. Originally published by the Hakluyt Society (London, 1881).

60 **Elisha Kent Kane and the seafaring frontier.**
Jeannette Mirsky. Boston: Little, Brown, 1954. 201p. map. bibliog.
A biography of the physician and naval officer who was one of the American pioneers of Arctic explorations. In the course of his voyages (1850-57), he charted unknown regions of Greenland, surveyed botany, geology, and meteorology, and studied the life of the Eskimo.

61 **The polar passion: the quest for the north pole, with selections from Arctic journals.**
Farley Mowat. Boston: Little, Brown, 1967; Toronto: McClelland & Stewart, 1967. 303p. maps. bibliog.
The author provides a brief introduction to eight excerpts from journals of Arctic explorers, including a selection on p. 197–222 from Fridtjof Nansen's *First crossing of Greenland* (q.v.). There are many interesting drawings and photographs.

62 **The first crossing of Greenland.**
Fridtjof Nansen. London: Longmans, Green, 1890. 2 vols. maps.
The official narrative of a difficult journey across the inland ice from the east coast to
the west coast of Greenland in the summer of 1888. Also included are summaries of
the scientific work of the expedition, and descriptions of Eskimo life.

63 **Greenland, the adjacent seas, and the North-West Passage to the Pacific
Ocean, illustrated in a voyage to Davis's strait during the summer of
1817.**
Bernard O'Reilly. New York: James Eastburn, 1818. 251p. maps.
A chronicle of a voyage to Greenland waters in 1817, with observations on the history
of Greenland, its Eskimos, the Arctic ice, and Arctic zoology.

64 **Northward over the 'great ice': a narrative of life and work along the
shores and upon the interior ice-cap of northern Greenland in the years
1886 and 1891-1897.**
Robert E. Peary. London: Methuen; New York: Frederick A. Stokes,
1898. 2 vols. maps.
The famous explorer chronicles in detail his four North Greenland expeditions from
1886 to 1897 and summarizes their results and discoveries. Peary's expeditions reached
points farther north than earlier explorers had attained. It is usually considered that his
journeys demonstrated the insularity of Greenland, a fact then disputed by some
explorers who considered the island to be part of a great Arctic continent. There are
many contemporary photographs.

65 **Dark companion.**
Bradley Robinson. New York: Robert M. McBride, 1947. map.
A fictionalized biography of Matthew Henson, the Afro-American who accompanied
Peary to the North Pole, including their 1895 trek by sledge and dog teams across
northern Greenland's icy wastes.

66 **Arctic whalers, icy seas: narratives of the Davis Strait whale fishery.**
W. Gillies Ross. Toronto: Irwin, 1985. 263p. map. bibliog.
A collection of first-hand narratives about whale fishery, especially about hunting the
Greenland or bowhead whale in the Davis Strait between Greenland and Baffin Island
during the nineteenth century. Introductions and commentaries are provided for each
chapter.

67 **An account of the Arctic regions, with a history and description of the
northern whale-fishery. Volume 1: The Arctic. Volume 2: The whale-
fishery.**
William Scoresby. Newton Abbot, England: David & Charles, 1969.
The first volume describes the geography, hydrography, meteorology, and zoology
found by exploring expeditions in the seas around Greenland. Volume two provides an
extensive report on Arctic whaling in the Greenland Sea and the Davis Strait. This is a
reprint of the original edition which was published by Archibald Constable
(Edinburgh, 1820).

68 **The Arctic regions: their situation, appearances, climate, and zoology.**
    William Scoresby.   London: The Religious Tract Society, 1820. 192p.
An early explorer describes Greenland's geographical features, climate and temperatures, icebergs and icefields, and zoology. Perhaps the most interesting part is his depiction of the variety of wildlife: whales, narwhals, dolphin, walrus, seals, foxes, polar bears, birds, and fishes.

69 **Journal of a voyage to the northern whale-fishery including researches and discoveries on the eastern coast of west Greenland made in the summer of 1822 in the ship Baffin of Liverpool.**
    William Scoresby, Jr.   Whitby, England: Caedmon of Whitby, 1980.
    472p. map.
Along with his pursuit of whales in Arctic waters, the author also mapped the coasts and carried on scientific investigations of the plants and animals, geology, and meteorology of eastern Greenland. The book supplements the volume by the author's father, *An account of the Arctic regions* (q.v.). Originally printed in Edinburgh (Archibald Constable) and London (Hurst Robinson) in 1823.

70 **Nansen, the explorer.**
    Edward Shackleton.   London: H. F. & G. Witherby, 1959. 209p. maps.
A brief, straightforward biography of the famed explorer, with accounts of his various expeditions to Greenland.

71 **Greenland voyager.**
    Tom and Cordelia Stamp.   Whitby, England: Caedmon of Whitby,
    1983. 191p.
An account of William Scoresby's years in the Greenland trade, compiled from excerpts from his journals. The book describes the life of the whaling men and the dangers of sea, ice, and fog. Scoresby was probably the best-known of the whaling captains in the early years of the nineteenth century.

72 **William Scoresby: Arctic scientist.**
    Tom and Cordelia Stamp.   Whitby, England: Caedmon of Whitby,
    1976. 253p. bibliog.
A biography of the man who, during part of his busy life, was a whaling captain, an Arctic explorer and surveyor, and a pioneer Arctic scientist. Many of his voyages took him to Greenland and its waters.

73 **Peary: the explorer and the man. Based on his personal papers.**
    John Edward Weems.   New York: Houghton Mifflin; London: Eyre &
    Spottiswoode, 1967. 362p. map. bibliog.
A biography of Admiral Robert Peary that includes an extended discussion of his Greenland expeditions in the 1890s. Peary's explorations added to the knowledge of northern Greenland and prepared him for his later assault on the North Pole, attained in 1909.

Arctic researches and life among the Esquimaux: being the narrative of an expedition in search of Sir John Franklin, in the years 1860, 1861, and 1862.
See item no. 226.

Fridtjof Nansen: Arctic explorer.
See item no. 342.

Hans the Eskimo: his story of Arctic adventures with Kane, Hayes, and Hall.
See item no. 344.

20th century

74   **Arctic odyssey: the life of Rear Admiral Donald B. Macmillan.**
Everett S. Allen.   New York: Dodd and Mead, 1962. 340p. maps.
The biography of an Arctic explorer who accompanied Peary on his North Pole expedition in 1908-09. In his own later investigations he surveyed and mapped, made tidal observations, studied the geology, botany, and ethnology of North Greenland, and aided in the construction of American airfields and radar stations during the Second World War.

75   **Watkin's last expedition.**
F. Spencer Chapman.   London: Chatto & Windus, 1934. 291p.
In 1933 H. G. Watkin lost his life in an expedition to explore the Greenland areas north of Ammassalik. This is an account of that tragedy and of the scientific and survey work conducted by the other members of the party.

76   **Polar exploration.**
Andrew Croft.   London: A. & C. Black, 1947. 2nd ed. 268p. maps. bibliog.
A general survey of north and south polar explorations. Chapter two on Greenland examines the Mylius–Ericksen expedition of 1906-08, the *Alabama* expedition of 1909-12, and Rasmussen's first Thule expedition in 1912.

77   **The 'Teddy' expedition: among the ice floes of Greenland.**
Kai R. Dahl, translated from the Danish by Grace Isabel Colbron.
New York; London: D. Appleton, 1925. 288p. map.
An account of the ill-fated voyage of the schooner *Teddy* in 1923, its wreck in the polar ice off eastern Greenland, and the crew's struggle to survive. The tale is told by a newspaperman who accompanied the expedition, the purpose of which was to hunt polar foxes.

78 **I sailed with Rasmussen.**
Peter Freuchen, translated from the Danish by Arnold Andersen. New York: Julian Messner, 1958. 224p. maps.
An informal biography of the noted Danish explorer Knud Rasmussen, related by the author through the story of their joint ventures in trade and travel among the polar Eskimos of Greenland and northern Canada.

79 **Mid-ice: the story of the Wegener expedition to Greenland.**
Johannes Georgi, translated from the German by F. H. Lyon. London: K. Paul, Trench, Trubner, 1934; New York: E. P. Dutton, 1935. 247p. map.
Based on the diaries and letters of one of its participants, the story unfolds of the ill-fated Wegener expedition, in which fatigue and exposure brought death to Alfred Wegener during a 150-mile winter journey from a central weather station to the coast.

80 **Exploring about the north pole of the winds.**
William Herbert Hobbs. New York and London: G. P. Putnam's Sons, 1930. 376p. maps.
The director of three University of Michigan expeditions to Greenland in 1926-28 focuses more on the rigours of scientific exploration in the far north than on the findings of their research on Arctic wind currents.

81 **Bartlett, the great Canadian explorer.**
Harold Horwood. Garden City, New York: Doubleday, 1977. 194p. maps. bibliog.
The biography of Robert Bartlett (1875-1946), an Arctic explorer for more than fifty years, who led scientific expeditions to Greenland and other northern areas.

82 **East of the great glacier.**
Helge Ingstad. New York: Alfred A. Knopf, 1937. 271p. maps.
The book relates the author's experiences as governor of Eirik Raudes Land in eastern Greenland (1932-33) and as leader of an exploring and trapping expedition, hunting for polar bears.

83 **Brief history of polar exploration since the introduction of flying.**
W. L. G. Joerg. New York: American Geographical Society, 1930. 2nd ed. 95p. maps. bibliog. (Special Publication No. 11).
In his discussion of the role of aviation in exploring and mapping polar regions, the author reviews briefly the four Greenland expeditions of the University of Michigan (1926-28) and the German and British expeditions of 1930.

84 **Those Greenland days.**
Martin Lindsay. Edinburgh; London: William Blackwood, 1932. maps.
The Greenland experiences of a member of the British Arctic Air Route Expedition of 1931. The objective of the group was a thorough meteorological and geographical survey of central Greenland, the least-known part of a proposed route from London to

Winnipeg. The book's focus is the author's personal experiences, however, rather than the scientific accomplishments of the study.

85 **Lost in the Arctic: being the story of the 'Alabama' expedition, 1909-1912.**
Ejnar Mikkelsen.   London: William Heinemann, 1913. 400p.
In 1909-12 the author headed a Danish expedition to eastern Greenland to search for survivors of a 1907 expedition. His ship, the *Alabama*, was wrecked, and the party had to await rescue. Mikkelsen tells of their vicissitudes, and his account affords many descriptions of their ice journeys and the natural history of that part of Greenland.

86 **Women of the four winds.**
Elizabeth Fagg Olds.   Boston: Houghton Mifflin, 1985. 318p. maps. bibliog.
Included (p. 231-96) in these biographies of famous women is the story of Louise Arner Boyd (1887-1972), who conceived, financed, and led seven scientific explorations of Greenland.

87 **Greenland by the polar sea: the story of the Thule expedition from Melville Bay to cape Morris Jessup.**
Knud Rasmussen, translated from the Danish by Asta and Rowland Kenney.   London: William Heinemann, 1921. 327p. maps.
Knud Rasmussen was a noted polar explorer and a man thoroughly familiar with Greenland. His 1916 expedition to North Greenland, which surveyed and mapped hitherto unknown parts of the coast, was notable for its use of Eskimo techniques of travel and hunting. Also discussed is the ethnography of the northern area, with many illustrations, and there are appendixes on the flora and fauna of the north coast by C. H. Ostenfeld and on its geology by Lauge Koch.

88 **Target: Arctic: men in the skies at the top of the world.**
George Simmons.   Philadelphia, New York: Chilton; Toronto: Ambassador, 1965. 420p. maps. bibliog.
A chronicle of the men and women who pioneered exploration of the Arctic by air. There are a number of references to flights over Greenland and a lengthier discussion of aviation in Greenland during the Second World War. Also included as appendix four is a 1933 memo prepared by Charles A. Lindbergh, assessing the advantages and disadvantages of a transatlantic air route by way of Greenland and Iceland.

89 **North ice: the British North Greenland expedition.**
C. J. W. Simpson.   London: Hodder & Stoughton, 1957. 384p. maps.
The author, who led a Royal Society and government-backed scientific expedition to Greenland in 1952-54, relates the story of its efforts and the geological, glaciological, and meteorological studies that were conducted.

90   **Vikings, Scots and Scraelings.**
      Myrtle Simpson.   London: Victor Gollancz, 1977. 189p. maps.
A narrative of a canoe journey along Greenland's southwest coast, with its participants
trying to discern the fate of the early Viking settlers and to investigate their relations
with the 'skrellings' (as the Vikings called the Eskimos).

91   **Discovery: the autobiography of Vilhjalmur Stefansson.**
      Vilhjalmur Stefansson.   New York, Toronto, London: McGraw-Hill,
      1964. 411p. maps.
The autobiography of one of the best known writers on Arctic explorations and
Eskimo life. His principal explorations were in the Canadian Arctic before the First
World War, and he visited Greenland only in the summer of 1953 at the invitation of
the Danish government. Stefansson notes his admiration for the Danes because of their
non-exploitative treatment of the Greenlanders.

92   **Mischief in Greenland.**
      H. W. Tilman.   London: Hollis & Carter, 1964. 192p. map.
An account of two mountaineering expeditions to southwest Greenland in 1961 and
1962.

93   **Triumph and tribulation.**
      H. W. Tilman.   Lymington, England: Nautical, 1977. 153p. maps.
The tale of two journeys to Greenland in a fifty-foot cutter, the first along the west
coast beyond the Arctic circle and the second ending in near-tragedy in the ice around
the east coast.

94   **Greenland journey: the story of Wegener's German expedition to
      Greenland in 1930-31 as told by members of the expedition and leader's
      diary.**
      Edited by Else Wegener, Fritz Loewe.   London; Glasgow: Blackie,
      1939. 295p. maps.
In 1930 Alfred Lothar Wegener led an expedition whose goal was to establish a station
on the Greenland ice sheet for scientific experiments in measurement. The story of his
death and the party's experiences are related by several members of the expedition and
through Wegener's diary.

95   **The man on the ice cap: the life of August Courtauld.**
      Nicholas Wollaston.   London: Constable, 1980. 260p.
The biography of a member of the British Arctic Air Route Expedition of 1930-31,
who was marooned alone on the Greenland ice cap for five months at his own choice.
He endured winter storms and the pains of frostbite while he experienced the pleasures
of solitude.

Arctic adventure: my life in the frozen north.
See item no. 221.

Geography and Geology

Geography

96 **The circumpolar north: a political and economic geography of the Arctic and sub-Arctic.**
Terence Armstrong.   London: Methuen; New York: Wiley, 1978. 303p. maps. bibliog.
Greenland's geography is seen in the general context of Arctic and sub-Arctic geography in the first chapter, while chapter five provides a survey of the island's physical features, history, social and economic conditions, and government. Chapter seven discusses the oceans around Greenland and other northern lands, and chapter eight examines the area's importance in world affairs.

97 **Stauning's Alps – Greenland: Scoresby Land and Nathorsts Land.**
Donald J. Bennet.   Reading, England: Gaston's Alpine Books & West Col, 1972. 120p. maps. bibliog.
Intended for climbers and mountaineers, this book discusses the geography, mountains, and flora and fauna of western Greenland's peninsular region. It also contains practical advice on planning, food, and equipment for mountaineering expeditions.

98 **The fiord region of East Greenland.**
Louise Arner Boyd.   New York: American Geographical Society, 1935. 369p. maps. (Special Publication No. 18).
The report of a 1933 expedition for scientific studies of glacial marginal features in the fjord area of eastern Greenland. It includes reports on physiographic and botanical studies, as well as an historical outline of the explorations of the region.

99   **The polar regions: a physical and economic geography of the Arctic and Antarctic.**
R. N. Rudmose Brown.   New York: E. P. Dutton, 1927. 245p. maps. bibliog.

An attempt to bring together basic information on the Arctic and Antarctic, drawn from the scientific reports of many polar expeditions. Greenland is included in the general discussion of such topics as exploration, colonization, polar climates, ice sheets and glaciers, vegetation and animal life, the Eskimo, whaling, and commercial and political aspects.

100   **Eskimo settlements in northeast Greenland.**
Peter Vilhelm Glob.   Copenhagen: Commission for Scientific Investigation in Greenland, 1946. 40p. bibliog. (Reports on Greenland, vol. 144, no. 6).

A list and description of 213 Eskimo settlements in northeastern Greenland, observed by various Arctic expeditions between 1823 and 1946.

101   **The Arctic seas: climatology, oceanography, geology, and biology.**
Edited by Yvonne Herman.   New York: Van Nostrand Reinhold, 1989. 888p. maps. bibliog.

Greenland and the Greenland Sea are considered throughout this collection of interdisciplinary studies by Western and Soviet scientists. Topics relating to Greenland include Arctic crustacea, phytoplankton, molluscs, glaciation, and sediment cores. The studies are broad in coverage; none focus solely on Greenland.

102   **Two cartographers.**
Halldór Hermannson.   New York: Kraus, 1966. 44p. maps. (*Islandica*, vol. XVII).

A brief discussion of the lives and maps of two early Icelandic cartographers, one of whom, Bishop Gudbrandur, made one of the first maps of Greenland in 1606. First edition published by Cornell University Library (Ithaca, New York, 1966).

103   **The Nordic seas.**
Edited by Burton G. Hurdle.   New York; Berlin; Heidelberg; Tokyo: Springer-Verlag, 1986. 777p. maps. bibliog.

A comprehensive multidisciplinary scientific description of the Greenland and Norwegian Seas, the western part of the Barents Sea, and the seas around Iceland, with many photographs. Included are sections on the history of scientific exploration of the Nordic seas, climate and atmospheric physics, characteristics of the ice cover and the sea ice, the physical oceanography of the seas and the seafloor, and the geophysics of the crust.

104 **Geography of the northlands.**
Edited by George H. T. Kimble, Dorothy Good. London: Chapman
& Hall; New York: American Geographical Society and John Wiley,
1955. 534p. maps.

Covers the Arctic and sub-Arctic areas, with general chapters on physiography, ice and
water masses, weather and climate, biogeography and marine life, aboriginal and
immigrant populations, transport, resources and economic development, political and
strategic aspects. Chapter eighteen (p. 372-86) by P. E. Uren deals specifically with
Greenland.

105 **The place names of North Greenland.**
Dan Laursen. Copenhagen: C. A. Reitzels Forlag, 1972. 443p. maps.
bibliog.

A comprehensive discussion of the names given to the geographical features of North
Greenland. The Arctic expeditions that explored the northern area from 1616 to 1960
are briefly identified, along with the place names that each expedition contributed.
This appeared as part of *Meddelelser on Grønland*, vol. 180, no. 2 (q.v.).

106 **The Poles.**
Willy Ley and the editors of Time-Life Books. Alexandria, Virginia:
Time-Life Books, 1980. rev. ed. 192p. bibliog.

Profusely illustrated in colour and black-and-white, the book affords a general look at
the Arctic and the Antarctic, with a number of references to Greenland's discovery,
geography, people, and animals.

107 **Arctic heritage: proceedings of a symposium. August 24-28, 1985. Banff,
Alberta, Canada.**
Edited by J. G. Nelson, Roger Needham, Linda Norton. Ottawa:
Association of Canadian Universities for Northern Studies (ACUNS),
1987. 653p. maps. bibliog.

There are many references to Greenland in the papers presented at this symposium on
the use and conservation of the natural and cultural heritage of the north. Two papers
treat Greenland topics specifically: 'Human implications of Arctic animal population
fluctuations: caribou in Greenland' by M. Meldgaard (p. 242-51) and 'Protected areas
and national parks in Greenland' by Henning Meyer (p. 567-75).

108 **An historical and descriptive account of Iceland, Greenland and the
Faroe Islands, with illustrations of their natural history.**
James Nicol. Edinburgh: Oliver & Boyd; London: Simpkin, Marshall,
1840. 416p. maps.

Depicts the scenery, geography, geology, history, flora and fauna, and peoples of
'three of the most singular and interesting countries on the face of the earth'. The
author was much interested in Greenland's Eskimos, whom he found indolent,
sociable, and peaceful.

109 **The geography of the polar regions consisting of a general characterization of polar nature by Otto Nordenskjöld and a regional geography of the Arctic and the Antarctic by Ludwig Mecking.**
Otto Nordenskjöld, Ludwig Mecking. New York: American Geographical Society, 1928. 359p. maps. bibliog.
Nordenskiöld provides a general description of Arctic and Antarctic climate, ice, soils and landforms, vegetation, and animal life. Mecking's two chapters on Greenland (p. 233-79) cover history, topography, geology, climate, plants and animals, and people.

110 **The Scandinavian world.**
Andrew C. O'Dell. London: Longmans, Green, 1957. 549p. maps. bibliog.
A solid geographical review of the Scandinavian world, including Greenland. It provides a physical and historical introduction and an extensive discussion of the economic geography (resources, mining, fuel and power, transportation, population, commerce and trade).

111 **Problems of polar research: a series of papers by thirty-one authors.**
New York: American Geographical Society, 1928. 479p. maps. (Special Publication No. 7).
Papers by leading students of polar problems give insights into the region's geography, climate, geology, ice cover, flora and fauna, Eskimo culture, and resources. None of the papers deals specifically with Greenland, but many of them contain references to the island.

112 **The Arctic basin.**
Edited by John E. Sater. Washington, DC: Arctic Institute of North America, 1969. 337p. maps. bibliog.
Greenland and other Arctic areas are considered within the context of this overall survey of the Arctic basin's oceanography, land masses, atmosphere, electrical properties, population, transportation, communications, construction, and living conditions.

113 **Arctic environment and resources.**
John E. Sater, A. G. Ronhovde, L. C. Van Allen. Washington, DC: Arctic Institute of North America, 1971. 309p. maps.
Contains general information on the geography, geology, and resources of the Arctic lands, with a very brief summary of Greenland's mineral resources (p. 288-90).

114 **Polar deserts and modern man.**
Edited by Terah L. Smiley, James H. Zumberge. Tucson, Arizona:
University of Arizona Press, 1974. 173p. maps. bibliog.
A collection of papers presented at the Polar Deserts Symposium of the American
Association for the Advancement of Science in 1971. The discussion of the physical
and biological features of the ice deserts of the Arctic and Antarctic contains frequent
references to Greenland.

115 **A geography of Norden: Denmark, Finland, Iceland, Norway, Sweden.**
Edited by Axel Sømme. London: Heinemann, 1968. 354p. maps.
bibliog.
Scandinavian geographers examine the region as a whole, as well as the individual
nations. For Denmark, Axel Schou and Kristian Antonsen consider geology,
landscapes, coastal features, soils, climate and vegetation, settlement and population,
agriculture, forestry and fisheries, industry, communications and trade, Greenland,
and the Faroe Islands. There are many photographs, maps, diagrams, and charts.

116 **Arctic and Antarctic: a modern geographical synthesis.**
David Sugden. Oxford: Basil Blackwell; Totowa, New Jersey: Barnes
& Noble, 1982. 472p. maps. bibliog.
This volume analyses Arctic and Antarctic geography, focusing on the interaction of
man and environment. Greenland is included in a general discussion of geographical
features and environmental change, with these features and the island's human
geography discussed in more specific terms in a separate chapter (p. 247-79).

117 **To the Arctic: an introduction to the Far Northern world.**
Steven B. Young. New York: John Wiley, 1988. 354p. bibliog.
The director of Vermont's Center for Northern Studies provides a comprehensive
portrait of the Arctic areas, including Greenland. Explored are the region's physical
characteristics, flora and fauna, history, and peoples.

Greenland.
See item no. 2.

The Arctic.
See item no. 4.

Greenland.
See item no. 5.

Handbook of North American Indians. Volume 5. Arctic.
See item no. 8.

North, Central and South America: Atlantic Islands.
See item no. 11.

Greenland: past and present.
See item no. 14.

Greenland.
See item no. 23.

Greenland.
See item no. 24.

Doctor Kane of the Arctic seas.
See item no. 50.

An account of the Arctic regions, with a history and description of the northern whale-fishery. Volume 1: The Arctic. Volume 2: The whale-fishery.
See item no. 67.

The Arctic regions: their situation, appearances, climate, and zoology.
See item no. 68.

Danish Greenland: its people and products.
See item no. 240.

The Eskimos: their environment and folkways.
See item no. 244.

Greenland: island at the top of the world.
See item no. 323.

Greenland in story and pictures.
See item no. 325.

Iceland and Greenland.
See item no. 343.

Atlases and gazetteers

118 **Gazetteer of Greenland: names approved by the United States Board on Geographic Names.**
Charles M. Heyda, Edward S. Szymanski.   Washington, DC:
Department of the Interior, 1983. 2nd ed. 271p.
Some 11,000 entries of places and features in Greenland, with listings of latitudes and longitudes for each one. The new spellings of some names reflect the phonemically-based orthography approved by the Ministry for Greenland in 1973.

119 **Danmark atlas.** (Atlas of Denmark.)
Edited by Johannes Humlum, Knud Nygård.   Copenhagen:
Gyldendal, 1976. 2nd ed. 40p. maps.
Twenty-six maps in colour, describing the physical nature, economy, population and communications of Denmark, Greenland and the Faroes. The explanatory text is in Danish.

120 **Arctic pilot.**
Hydrographer of the Navy, Great Britain.   Taunton, England: The
Author, 1975-85. 3 vols. maps.
These navigational guides also include much information about climate and weather,
history, and other topics. Volume two includes the east coast of Greenland and volume
three the west and northwest coasts. Supplements are published regularly to update the
volumes.

121 **Polar regions atlas.**
Washington, DC: Central Intelligence Agency, Government Printing
Office, 1978. 66p. maps.
An atlas of the Arctic and Antarctic polar regions, with brief but useful information on
geography, climate, population, economic development, natural resources, environmental protection, science programmes, and sovereignty problems. Small maps show
most of these features for Greenland, and there are large maps of both polar areas.
The atlas also contains a gazetteer/index of populated places, islands, hydrographic and
physiographic features, and administrative divisions.

122 **Picture atlas of the Arctic.**
Ragnar Thorén.   Amsterdam: Elsevier, 1969. 449p. maps. bibliog.
A discussion of the geography of the Arctic region. Chapter five on Greenland (p. 177-
212) describes briefly the landscape, ice sheet and glaciers, mineral resources, and
transportation and illustrates them with numerous black-and-white photographs.

Geology

123 **Glaciological research on the North Atlantic coasts.**
Hans W:son Ahlmann.   London: The Royal Geographical Society,
1948. 83p. maps. (R.G.S. Research Series No. 1).
Covering glaciological research conducted from 1918 to 1946 in land areas surrounding
the Northern Atlantic, the book includes studies of the glaciers of Clavering Island in
northeast Greenland.

124 **The coast of northeast Greenland, with hydrographic studies in the
Greenland Sea.**
Louise Arner Boyd. New York: American Geographical Society, 1948.
339p. maps.
The investigations of glacial geology, flora, and hydrographical and topographical
surveys, by expeditions to northeast Greenland in 1937 and 1938.

125   **Arctic geology and geophysics: proceedings of the third international symposium on Arctic geology.**
Edited by Ashton F. Embry, Hugh R. Balkwill.   Calgary, Alberta:
Canadian Society of Petroleum Geologists, 1982. 552p. maps. bibliog.

The geology of Greenland is one of the topics discussed in this collection of papers on the resources of the Arctic. The principal focus is exploration for, and exploitation of, mineral resources.

126   **Geology of Greenland.**
Edited by Arthur Escher, W. Stuart Watt.   Copenhagen: Geological
Survey of Greenland, 1976. 603p. maps. bibliog.

A comprehensive survey of the geology of Greenland, with chapters by experts on the principal geological aspects: stratigraphy, economic geology, glaciation, minerals, coal and petroleum geology, fossil flora, palaeovertebrate fauna.

127   **Frozen assets of the ice cores.**
Richard Fifield.   *New Scientist*, vol. 118, no. 1608 (April 14, 1988),
p. 28-29.

Explains why glaciologists and climatologists find the huge ice sheets of Greenland and the Antarctic to be valuable records of the earth's previous atmospheres.

128   **Do diatoms beneath the Greenland ice sheet indicate interglacials warmer than present?**
David M. Harwood.   *Arctic*, vol. 39, no. 4 (December 1986),
p. 304-08. bibliog.

The author examined basal sediment debris from the Greenland ice sheet and discovered the presence of common freshwater and rare marine diatoms. This suggests a warmer and/or longer interglacial period than the present Holocene 'interglacial'.

129   **Icebergs: a bibliography relevant to eastern Canadian waters.**
Edited by L. M. Howard.   Calgary, Alberta: Arctic Institute of North
America, 1986. 277p. (Environmental Studies Revolving Funds Report
030).

An annotated listing of more than 1,100 citations on icebergs, with the west coast of Greenland as one of the areas included.

130   **Geophysics of the polar regions.**
Edited by E. S. Husebye, G. L. Johnson, Y. Kristoffersen.
Amsterdam: Elsevier, 1985. 470p. maps. bibliog. (Reprinted from
Tectonophysics, vol. 114, nos. 1-4).

Among the papers presented to the symposium were two dealing with the motion of Greenland relative to Ellesmere Island along Nares Strait: 'Nares Strait – a suture zone: geophysical and geological implications' by H. Ruth Jackson (p. 11-28, maps, bibliog.) and 'Evolution of the Eurasian Basin and its implications to the motion of Greenland along Nares Strait' by S. P. Srivastava (p. 29-53, maps, bibliog.).

131 **Greenland ice core: geophysics, geochemistry, and the environment.**
Edited by C. C. Langway, Jr., H. Oeschger, W. Dansgaard.
Washington, DC: American Geophysical Union, 1985. 118p. maps.
bibliog. (Geophysical Monograph 33).

This major achievement in glaciology is a collection of seventeen scientific studies of
ice cores from the surface of the Greenland ice sheet. It represents a systematic effort
to determine the geophysical and geochemical characteristics of the ice sheet and to
examine its climatic record.

132 **Placers of cosmic dust in the blue ice lakes of Greenland.**
M. Maurette, C. Hammer, D. E. Brownlee, N. Reeh, H. H.
Thomsen. *Science*, vol. 233 (22 August 1986). p. 869-72.

A concentration process in the melt zone of the Greenland ice cap has produced the
richest known deposit of cosmic dust on the earth's surface. These extraterrestrial
particles are well-preserved and include some not found in deep-sea samples.

133 **Sulfate and nitrate concentrations from a South Greenland ice core.**
P. A. Mayewski, W. B. Lyons, M. J. Spencer, M. Twickler, W.
Dansgaard, B. Koci, C. I. Davidson, R. E. Honrath. *Science*, vol. 232
(23 May 1986). p. 975-77.

A report on research findings from an ice core in South Greenland covering the period
1869 to 1894. The data show a tripling of excess sulphate concentration since 1900-10
and a doubling of nitrate concentration since 1955. The increases may be attributable
to airborne deposits from the burning of fossil fuel and biomass in North America and
Eurasia.

134 **The ocean basins and margins. Volume 5. The Arctic Ocean.**
Edited by Alan E. M. Nairn, Michael Churkin, Jr., Francis G. Stehli.
New York; London: Plenum, 1981. 672p. bibliog.

Chapter five by Peter Dawes and John S. Peel (p. 201-64) is a detailed examination of
the geology of the northern margin of Greenland from Baffin Bay to the Greenland
Sea. Chapter eleven by P. R. Vogt, R. K. Perry, R. H. Feder, H. S. Fleming, and N.
Z. Cherkis (p. 493-598) considers the geology and geophysics of the Greenland–
Norwegian Sea and Iceland. There is an extensive bibliography for each chapter.

135 **Arctic geology: proceedings of the second international symposium on
Arctic geology, held February 1-4, 1971, at San Francisco, California.**
Edited by Max G. Pitcher. Tulsa, Oklahoma: American Association
of Petroleum Geologists, 1973. 747p. maps.

Includes papers on the development of the Precambrian Shield in West Greenland, the
pre-Quaternary history of North Greenland, the Mesozoic geology of East Greenland,
the Tertiary of Greenland, the Caledonian geology of the Scoresby Sund region of
Central East Greenland, Devonian stratigraphy, the economics of petroleum
exploration and production in the Arctic, and Arctic geopolitics.

136 **Geology of the Arctic: proceedings of the first international symposium on Arctic geology.**
Edited by Gilbert O. Raasch. Toronto: University of Toronto Press, 1961. 2 vols. maps.

Includes twenty-one papers on aspects of Greenland's geology, four papers on glaciological investigations of the island, and one paper on the history of geological studies in Greenland.

137 **Soils of the polar landscapes.**
John C. F. Tedrow. New Brunswick, New Jersey: Rutgers University Press, 1977. 638p. maps. bibliog.

The book offers a comprehensive description of polar soils in both Arctic and Antarctic regions. After general discussions of climate, biotic factors, permafrost, weathering, soil classifications, and geographic zones, there are chapters on individual countries or regions. The chapter on Greenland discusses climate, vegetation, and the differing types of soil in the various parts of the island.

138 **Greenland icefields and life in the North Atlantic, with a new discussion of the causes of the Ice Age.**
G. Frederick Wright, Warren Upham. New York: D. Appleton, 1896. 407p. maps.

The authors are most concerned with Greenland's inland ice and what it tells the scientist about the ice ages, but they also describe the island's Eskimos, plants, and animals. Their trip to Greenland occurred in the summer of 1894.

139 **Growth of Greenland ice sheet: interpretation.**
H. Jay Zwally. *Science*, vol. 246 (22 December 1989), p. 1589- 91.

Increased thickening of the Greenland ice sheet may be explained by higher precipitation than the long-term average. This may be a characteristic of warmer climates in the polar regions.

140 **Growth of Greenland ice sheet: measurement.**
H. Jay Zwally, Anita C. Brenner, Judy A. Major, Robert A. Bindschadler, James G. Marsh. *Science*, vol. 246 (22 December 1989), p. 1587-89.

Measurements of Greenland ice sheet elevation change by satellite altimetry indicate an increase in the thickness of the ice south of 72 degrees north latitude.

The national park in north-east Greenland.
See item no. 1.

Greenland: past and present.
See item no. 14.

An account of the Arctic regions, with a history and description of the northern whale-fishery. Volume 1: The Arctic. Volume 2: The whale-fishery.
See item no. 67.

Journal of a voyage to the northern whale-fishery including researches and discoveries on the eastern coast of west Greenland made in the summer of 1822 in the ship Baffin of Liverpool.
See item no. 69.

Greenland by the polar sea: the story of the Thule expedition from Melville Bay to cape Morris Jessup.
See item no. 87.

The fiord region of East Greenland.
See item no. 98.

The Arctic seas: climatology, oceanography, geology, and biology.
See item no. 101.

The Nordic seas.
See item no. 103.

An historical and descriptive account of Iceland, Greenland and the Faroe Islands, with illustrations of their natural history.
See item no. 108.

The geography of the polar regions consisting of a general characterization of polar nature by Otto Nordenskjöld and a regional geography of the Arctic and the Antarctic by Ludwig Mecking.
See item no. 109.

Problems of polar research: a series of papers by thirty-one authors.
See item no. 111.

Arctic environment and resources.
See item no. 113.

A geography of Norden: Denmark, Finland, Iceland, Norway, Sweden.
See item no. 115.

Flora and Fauna

141 **The Arctic and Antarctic: their division into geobotanical areas.**
V. D. Aleksandrova, translated from the Russian by Doris Löve.
Cambridge: Cambridge University Press, 1980. 247p. maps. bibliog.
A noted Soviet researcher, who has devoted her life to the study of vegetation above
the Arctic Circle, divides the Arctic into the tundra region and the region of the polar
deserts. There are frequent references to Greenland in the general discussion of plant
life.

142 **The flora of Greenland.**
Tyge W. Böcher, Kjeld Holmen, Knud Jakobsen, translated from the
Danish by T. T. Elkington, M. C. Lewis.   Copenhagen: P. Haase &
Son, 1968. 312p. map.
This illustrated manual of the vascular plants of Greenland lists and describes the
various species and the areas in which they may be found.

143 **Bibliography on Greenlandic botany.**
T. T. Böcher, K. Horskjaer.   In: *Arctica 1978: 7th Northern Libraries
Colloquy, 19-23 September 1978.* Edited by Sylvie Devers. Paris:
Éditions du Centre National de la Recherche Scientifique, 1982, p. 179-
82.
A bibliography that lists the main references on all aspects of Greenlandic botany from
the nineteenth century to the present.

144 **Arctic animals: a celebration of survival.**
Fred Bruemmer.   Toronto: McClelland & Stewart, 1986. 159p.
bibliog.
An introduction to the bird and animal life of the Arctic, including Greenland. Richly
illustrated by the author's colour and black-and-white photographs.

Flora and Fauna

145 **Encounters with Arctic animals.**
Fred Bruemmer.   Toronto: McGraw-Hill Ryerson, 1972. 254p.
bibliog.

A survey of the wildlife of the Arctic from Alaska to Greenland, as the author has
come to know it from personal experience. Depicted, with many colour and black-and-
white photographs by the author, are seals, polar bears, walruses, foxes, muskoxen,
birds, narwhals, whales, and sharks.

146 **The wolf (*canis lupus*) in Greenland: a historical review and present
status.**
Peter R. Dawes, Magnus Elander, Mats Ericson.   *Arctic*, vol. 39,
no. 2 (June 1986), p. 119-32. maps. bibliog.

Although Greenland's wolf population has been assumed to be in decline, there is
abundant evidence that a renewed inflow and dispersal of wolves from northern
Canada has been taking place in recent years. The wolf is reoccupying its former range
and by 1983 had reached the Scoresby Sund region.

147 **The seabirds of Greenland: their status and conservation.**
P. G. H. Evans.   In: *Status and conservation of the world's seabirds*.
Edited by J. P. Croxall, P. G. H. Evans, and R. W. Schreiber.
Cambridge, England: International Council for Bird Preservation,
1984. p. 49-84. maps. bibliog. (ICBP Technical Publication no. 2).

Twenty species of seabirds breed in Greenland, mainly on the west coast. Knowledge
of their population sizes is very scant, but there is good evidence of a major decline in
at least one species, the Brunnich's Guillemot, as a result of over-hunting and
entanglement in fish nets.

148 **Grønlands blomster/flowers of Greenland.**
Jon Feilberg, Bent Fredskild, Sune Holt.   Copenhagen: Forlaget
Regnbuen, 1984. 98p. map.

This volume describes and depicts in black-and-white illustrations some 500 species of
vascular plants found in Greenland. There are morphological descriptions and
chromosome numbers for the flowering plants and ferns, as well as information on
their distribution.

149 **The Arctic year.**
Peter Freuchen, Finn Salomonsen.   New York: G. P. Putnam's Sons,
1958. 438p. maps. bibliog.

A month-by-month account of life in the Arctic. Containing detailed descriptions of
the growth and adaptation of the flora and fauna, it also gives much attention to the
life of the Eskimo. Greenland is covered both in the general discussion and in many
specific references. Of particular interest are the descriptions of the seasonal
migrations of the Eskimos, their adaptation to the harsh climatic conditions, and their
great understanding of the animal life of the Arctic.

Flora and Fauna

150   In the land of the musk-ox: tales of wild life in northeast Greenland.
John Giaever, translated from the Danish by Munda Whittaker and
Walter Oliver.   London: Jarrolds, 1958. 191p.
The author relates his experiences as a hunter in Greenland.

151   Arctic life of birds and mammals, including man.
Laurence Irving.   Berlin; Heidelberg; New York: Springer-Verlag,
1972. 192p. maps. bibliog.
Examines the Arctic environment and its land and sea mammals and birds and
considers their adjustments to the climate and the maintenance of their populations.

152   Cytotaxonomical atlas of the Arctic flora.
Aksel Löve, Doris Löve.   Vaduz: J. Cramer, 1975. 598p. bibliog.
An extensive atlas and checklist of the families, genera, species, and subspecies of
vascular plants found in the northlands, including Greenland.

153   The Greenland caribou: zoogeography, taxonomy and population
dynamics.
Morten Meldgaard.   Copenhagen: Commission for Scientific Research
in Greenland, 1986. 88p. map. bibliog.
A comprehensive review of information on the caribou, the animal with the most
extensive historical record in Greenland. The caribou ranged over most of the island
but now is found only in southwestern Greenland and northernmost West Greenland.
This appeared in *Meddelelser om Grønland: Bioscience* no. 20.

154   Kingdom of the ice bear: a portrait of the Arctic.
Hugh Miles, Mike Salisbury.   Austin, Texas: University of Texas
Press, 1986. 223p. map.
A personal account by two members of the BBC Natural History Unit of their
experiences during two years filming in Greenland and other parts of the Arctic world.
The authors describe the ecology of the region and the sequence of seasonal events,
and show how flora, fauna, and man survive in the intense cold. Illustrated with many
full-colour photographs.

155   Swimmers and sea birds.
Robin Minion.   Edmonton, Alberta: University of Alberta, Boreal
Institute for Northern Studies, 1984. 79p. (BINS Bibliographic Series,
no. 12).
A bibliography on birds found in Greenland and other parts of the Arctic. Includes
short notes for many of the 201 references.

156 **Polar animals.**
Alwin Pedersen, translated from the French by Gwynne Vevers.
London: George G. Harrap, 1962; New York: Taplinger, 1966. 188p.
map.
A description of the fauna of northeast Greenland, based on six years of observation.
After a brief description of the area, the author devotes a chapter to each of its
principal animals: the musk-ox, the Arctic wolf, the Arctic fox, Arctic hares, the polar
bear, lemmings and ermine, the walrus, and seals. He also includes the most typical
birds: the ptarmigan, the red-throated diver, geese, sea birds, and birds of the uplands.

157 **The polar worlds.**
Richard Perry. New York: Taplinger, 1973. 316p. maps. bibliog. (The
Many Worlds of Wildlife Series, vol. 2).
Descriptions of mammals and birds of the Arctic and Antarctic, including those found
in Greenland: caribou, foxes, hares, ivory gulls, lemmings, muskoxen, polar bears,
walruses, and wolves.

158 **Polar bears: proceedings of the eighth working meeting of the IUCN/SSC
polar bear specialist group January 1981.**
Gland, Switzerland: International Union for Conservation of Nature
and Natural Resources, 1985. 151p.
Polar bears in Greenland is one of the topics covered in papers presented at the
conference of specialists on that animal in 1981.

159 **Circumpolar Arctic flora.**
Nicholas Polunin. Oxford: Clarendon Press, 1959. 514p. map. bibliog.
This volume, based in part on the author's field work in Greenland, Spitzbergen,
Canada, and Alaska, provides an extensive check-list and descriptions of the vascular
plants found in the Arctic.

160 **Arctic animal ecology.**
Hermann Remmert. Berlin; Heidelberg; New York: Springer-
Verlag, 1980. 250p. maps. bibliog.
Although the book is concerned mainly with ecological research on Spitzbergen, there
are a number of references to plant and animal life in Greenland.

161 **The Arctic and its wildlife.**
Bryan Sage, with specialist contributions from Hugh Danks, Eric
Haber, Peter G. Kevan, Thomas G. Smith. London: Croom Helm;
New York: Facts on File, 1986. 190p. maps. bibliog.
An extensive examination by specialists of the Arctic landscapes and oceans and the
plants, animals, birds, and insects that live there. The book provides an excellent
introduction to the flora and fauna of Greenland and is clearly written and beautifully
illustrated.

162 **Animals of the Arctic: the ecology of the far north.**
Bernard Stonehouse. London: Ward Lock; New York: Holt,
Rinehart, & Winston, 1971. 172p. maps. bibliog.

A presentation of animal life in Arctic and sub-Arctic regions, with full attention to
animals and birds found in Greenland and its waters, including musk-oxen, caribou,
Arctic hares, seals, polar bears, walruses, falcons, snow buntings. Lavishly illustrated
with colour photographs.

163 **Birds of the Atlantic ocean.**
Ted Stokes. New York: Macmillan, 1968. 156p. maps.

Includes descriptions, and pictures by Keith Shackleton, of birds found in coastal
Greenland: the dovekie, the razorbill, several species of guillemot, the puffin. the
kittiwake, and various species of gulls, skua, and phalarope.

164 **Birds of the Thule district, northwest Greenland.**
Richard Vaughan. *Arctic*, vol. 41, no. 1 (March 1988), p. 53-58.

A record of forty-seven species of birds observed in the Thule district from 1983 to
1986.

165 **Whales of the world: a handbook and field guide to all the living species
of whales, dolphins and porpoises.**
Lyall Watson. London: Hutchinson, 1985. 2nd ed. 303p. maps.
bibliog.

A comprehensive summary of the appearance, habits, and distribution of seventy-six
species of marine mammals, a number of which are found in Greenland waters. These
include the Arctic walrus, the narwhal, harp seals and ringed seals, as well as whales.

Flora and Fauna

Narrative of discovery and adventure in the polar seas and regions: with illustrations of their climate, geology, and natural history; and an account of the whale-fishery.
See item no. 58.

Greenland, the adjacent seas, and the North-West Passage to the Pacific Ocean, illustrated in a voyage to Davis's strait during the summer of 1817.
See item no. 63.

An account of the Arctic regions, with a history and description of the northern whale-fishery. Volume 1: The Arctic. Volume 2: The whale-fishery.
See item no. 67.

The Arctic regions: their situation, appearances, climate, and zoology.
See item no. 68.

Journal of a voyage to the northern whale-fishery including researches and discoveries on the eastern coast of west Greenland made in the summer of 1822 in the ship Baffin of Liverpool.
See item no. 69.

Greenland by the polar sea: the story of the Thule expedition from Melville Bay to cape Morris Jessup.
See item no. 87.

The circumpolar north: a political and economic geography of the Arctic and sub-Arctic.
See item no. 96.

Stauning's Alps – Greenland: Scoresby Land and Nathorsts Land.
See item no. 97.

The fiord region of East Greenland.
See item no. 98.

The polar regions: a physical and economic geography of the Arctic and Antarctic.
See item no. 99.

The Arctic seas: climatology, oceanography, geology, and biology.
See item no. 101.

Geography of the northlands.
See item no. 104.

The Poles.
See item no. 106.

Arctic heritage: proceedings of a symposium. August 24-28, 1985. Banff, Alberta, Canada.
See item no. 107.

An historical and descriptive account of Iceland, Greenland and the Faroe Islands, with illustrations of their natural history.
See item no. 108.

The geography of the polar regions consisting of a general characterization of polar nature by Otto Nordenskjöld and a regional geography of the Arctic and Antarctic by Ludwig Mecking.
See item no. 109.

Problems of polar research: a series of papers by thirty-one authors.
See item no. 111.

A geography of Norden: Denmark, Finland, Iceland, Norway, Sweden.
See item no. 115.

To the Arctic: an introduction to the far northern world.
See item no. 117.

The coast of northeast Greenland, with hydrographic studies in the Greenland Sea.
See item no. 124.

Soils of the polar landscapes.
See item no. 137.

Greenland icefields and life in the North Atlantic, with a new discussion of the causes of the Ice Age.
See item no. 138.

Recent archaeological investigations of West Greenland caribou hunting.
See item no. 170.

Eskimos.
See item no. 326.

Eskimos.
See item no. 338.

Arctic bibliography.
See item no. 375.

Prehistory and Archaeology

166 **The use of the sæter in medieval Norse farming in Greenland.**
Svend E. Albrethsen, Christian Keller. *Arctic Anthropology*, vol. 23, nos. 1-2 (1986), p. 91-107. map. bibliog.
A report on an intensive field survey, conducted 1974-79, of medieval Norse ruins in the Qordlortoq valley. It provides information on medieval agriculture and on the 'sæter', houses used in the summer when herds were shifted from pasture to pasture.

167 **Eskimo prehistory.**
Hans-Georg Bandi, translated by Ann E. Keep. London: Methuen, 1967; Seattle, Washington: University of Washington Press, 1969. 226p. maps. bibliog. (Studies of Northern Peoples, No. 2).
A survey of the prehistory of the Eskimos of Greenland, Alaska, and Canada, drawing upon the research of archaeologists and physical anthropologists. One section of the work (p. 157-74) deals specifically with sites, finds, and prehistoric cultures in Greenland.

168 **Archaeological investigations on Clavering Ø, northeast Greenland.**
Hans-Georg Bandi, Jørgen Meldgaard. Copenhagen: Commission for Scientific Investigation in Greenland, 1952. 85p. (Reports on Greenland, vol. 126, no. 4).
This report of a 1948 investigation of the ruins of twenty-five winter houses in a former Eskimo settlement in northeast Greenland includes descriptions of the ruins and artifacts found there and an examination of the cultural level of the aboriginal inhabitants.

169 **Arctic archaeology: a bibliography and history.**
Albert A. Dekin, Jr.   New York; London: Garland, 1978. 279p.
Provides a historical summary of the findings of Arctic archaeology from the days of
the early explorers to the excavations of the 1970s, as well as an extensive
archaeological bibliography with many citations of Greenland investigations.

170 **Recent archaeological investigations of West Greenland caribou hunting.**
Bjarne Grønnow. *Arctic Anthropology*, vol. 23, nos. 1-2 (1986),
p. 57-80. maps. bibliog.
This article reviews the research on caribou hunting in West Greenland, describes the
inland environment, and presents results from two recent archaeological projects.

171 **The mummies of Qilakitsoq.**
Jens P. Hart Hansen, Jørgen Meldgaard, Jørgen Nordqvist. *National
Geographic Magazine*, vol.167, no. 2 (February 1985), p. 190-207.
A report on the research on eight well-preserved Inuit bodies, dating from around
1475, found at an abandoned settlement on the west coast of Greenland. The authors
call their discovery 'one of the most valuable finds of human remains and clothing ever
made in the Arctic region'.

172 **Voyage to Greenland.**
Frederica de Laguna.   New York: W. W. Norton, 1977. 285p.
The story of the author's voyage to Greenland and her sojourn there in the summer of
1929 as assistant to the Danish explorer and archaeologist, Therkel Mathiassen. She
records the experiences of an anthropologist's first field trip, an archaeological
investigation of medieval Eskimo sites near Upernavik, the northernmost colony on
the west coast of Greenland. The book is composed mainly of her original journal
entries and letters to her family, describing the hardships of the research.

173 **Paleo-Eskimo Cultures in Disko Bugt, West Greenland.**
Helge Larsen, Jørgen Meldgaard.   Copenhagen: Commission for
Scientific Investigation in Greenland, 1958. 77p. (Reports on
Greenland, vol. 161, no. 2).
A historical survey of a Sermermiut Eskimo settlement in western Greenland, with a
discussion of the two different palaeo-Eskimo cultures whose artifacts were found in
the locality.

174 **Settlement and land use in the inner fjords of Godthaab district, West
Greenland.**
Thomas H. McGovern, Richard H. Jordan.   *Arctic Anthropology*, vol.
19, no. 1 (1982), p. 63-79. bibliog.
The findings of a 1981 Greenlandic – American archaeological survey project, focusing
on Norse land use and caribou exploitation in the fourteenth century but with
references to earlier and later patterns.

Prehistory and Archaeology

175 **Prehistory of the eastern Arctic.**
Moreau S. Maxwell. Orlando, Florida: Academic Press, 1985. 327p. maps. bibliog.
A detailed but quite readable discussion of the prehistoric peoples of the eastern Arctic, including those of Greenland, tracing the technologies, tactics, and strategies of the Arctic Eskimo over nearly 4,000 years.

176 **A contribution to paleoeskimo archaeology in Greenland.**
Tinna Møbjerg. *Arctic Anthropology*, vol. 23, nos. 1-2 (1986), p. 19-56. bibliog.
This study was based on surveys in 1977, 1981, 1982, and 1984 on Disko Island and in the Ammassalik district. It describes the present range and dating of five Greenlandic Palaeoeskimo cultures, classifies the settlement types, and compares these cultures with other finds in Greenland and with Canadian Palaeoeskimo cultures.

177 **Dog remains from a Palaeoeskimo settlement in West Greenland.**
Jeppe Møhl. *Arctic Anthropology*, vol. 23, nos. 1-2 (1986), p. 81-89. map. bibliog.
The study of dog bones from an excavation in West Greenland provides the first proof of the animal's existence in Palaeoeskimo times.

178 **Buried Norsemen at Herjolfsnes: an archaeological and historical study.**
Poul Nörlund. Copenhagen: [no publisher listed], 1924. 270p.
An exhaustive account of the archaeological findings at the excavation of a village in southern Greenland, with a catalogue and many photographs of the finds. The village was settled in the tenth century AD and lasted until the fifteenth century.

Handbook of North American Indians. Volume 5. Arctic.
See item no. 8.

Greenland.
See item no. 23.

Vikings!
See item no. 40.

Viking expansion westwards.
See item no. 41.

The heroic age of Scandinavia.
See item no. 48.

The history of Greenland. Vol. I. Earliest times to 1700. Vol. II. 1700-1782. Vol. III. 1782-1808.
See item no. 179.

Hunters of the polar north: the Eskimos.
See item no. 228.

Eskimos.
See item no. 333.

Arctic bibliography.
See item no. 375.

History

General

179 **The history of Greenland. Vol. I. Earliest times to 1700, Vol. II. 1700-1782, Vol. III. 1782-1808.**
Finn Gad. London: C. Hurst, 1970 (vol. I); Montreal: McGill-Queen's University Press, 1973, 1982 (vols. II, III). maps. bibliog.

In this comprehensive, detailed and solidly documented history of Greenland from the first inhabitants to 1808, the author's goal is to tell the total history of Greenland, and he may have succeeded. All aspects are included: political, demographic, economic, social, missionary efforts, scientific explorations, early settlers, Eskimo culture, archaeology. There are also many illustrations.

180 **Greenland.**
Vilhjalmur Stefansson. Garden City, New York: Doubleday Doran, 1942. 338p. map. bibliog.

A history of Greenland from prehistoric times to the Second World War, concerned mostly with the centuries of exploration. The author assesses the controversial theories of early discoveries of Greenland by Greeks in the fourth century BC, and Irish in the sixth century AD, and provides an extensive discussion of Viking Greenland from the days of Erik the Red to the disappearance of the Norse colonies in the fifteenth century.

181 **Changing Greenland.**
Geoffrey Williamson. New York: Library Publishers, 1954. 280p. maps. bibliog.

Traces the development of Greenland from Viking times to the immediate post-Second World War period and the adoption of the new Danish constitution in 1953. About half the book deals with postwar changes in administration, health care, the fishing industry, scientific explorations, and defence and security.

Greenland.
See item no. 2.

Handbook of North American Indians. Volume 5. Arctic.
See item no. 8.

North, Central and South America: Atlantic Islands.
See item no. 11.

Some characteristic problems in present-day Greenland.
See item no. 12.

Greenland: past and present.
See item no. 14.

Greenland.
See item no. 23.

The discoverers: an encyclopedia of explorers and exploration.
See item no. 26.

The scientific exploration of Greenland from the Norsemen to the present.
See item no. 29.

The lands of silence: a history of Arctic and Antarctic exploration.
See item no. 30.

Safe return doubtful: the heroic age of polar exploration.
See item no. 31.

To the Arctic! the story of northern exploration from earliest times to the present.
See item no. 32.

A history of polar exploration.
See item no. 33.

Eskimos and explorers.
See item no. 34.

The circumpolar north: a political and economic geography of the Arctic and sub-Arctic.
See item no. 96.

An historical and descriptive account of Iceland, Greenland and the Faroe Islands, with illustrations of their natural history.
See item no. 108.

The geography of the polar regions consisting of a general characterization of polar nature by Otto Nordenskjöld and a regional geography of the Arctic and the Antarctic by Ludwig Mecking.
See item no. 109.

To the Arctic: an introduction to the far northern world.
See item no. 117.

Greenland: island at the top of the world.
See item no. 323.

Iceland and Greenland.
See item no. 343.

The Vikings

182 **The decline of the Norse settlements in Greenland.**
Joel Berglund. *Arctic Anthropology*, vol. 23, nos. 1-2 (1986), p. 109-35. bibliog.

The article seeks to explain the reasons for the decline and fall of Norse settlements in Greenland and the fate of their inhabitants. Overexploitation of vegetational resources was perhaps an important factor.

183 **The lost colonies of Greenland.**
Fradley Garner. *Scandinavian Review*, vol. 67, no. 2 (June 1979), p. 39-47.

Considers the various theories about the sudden disappearance of medieval colonies of farmers and fishermen in Greenland.

184 **Land under the pole star: a voyage to the Norse settlements of Greenland and the saga of the people that vanished.**
Helge Ingstad, translated from the Norwegian by Naomi Walford.
London: Jonathan Cape; New York: St. Martin's, 1966. 381p. maps.

The description of a journey made in 1953 to study Greenland settlements founded by Erik the Red about AD 1000. The author presents the history, economic livelihood, archaeology, society and domestic life of the early dwellers.

185 **The Greenland trade-route.**
G. J. Marcus. *Economic History Review*, 2nd series, vol. 7, no. 1 (1954), p. 71-80.

Discusses the trade between Greenland and Norway from the eleventh century to the early fifteenth century. The Greenland settlements imported iron, tar, timber, and grain and exported walrus and narwhal tusks, sealskins, wadmal, falcons, and occasionally live polar bears.

186 **Westviking: the ancient Norse in Greenland and North America.**
Farley Mowat. Boston; Toronto: Little Brown, 1965. 494p. maps. bibliog.

A reconstruction of the Viking voyages of discovery and exploration to Greenland and North America, with detailed attention to the years between 960 and 1010 AD. Using information drawn from climatology, anthropology, zoology, seamanship, and the sagas, the author gives detailed pictures both of Erik the Red's voyage to Greenland in the tenth century and of Leif Ericsson's journey to Vinland in 1002–1003.

187 **Viking settlers in Greenland and their descendants during five hundred years.**
Poul Nørlund.   London: Cambridge University Press; Copenhagen: GEC Gads Forlag, 1936. 160p. bibliog.
A history of Norse settlements in Greenland and a description of the settlers' way of life from the tenth to the fifteenth centuries, based on archaeological research.

188 **Unsolved mysteries of the Arctic.**
Vilhjalmur Stefansson.   Freeport, New York: Books for Libraries Press, 1972. 381p. maps. bibliog.
One of the mysteries examined is the disappearance of the Greenland colony in the fifteenth or sixteenth century. No Scandinavian voyages to Greenland are recorded after 1410, and no settlers remained alive when ships again arrived later in the century. Among the possible explanations for the colony's demise are disease, famine or malnutrition, climatic change, or extermination by Eskimos. Originally printed in 1938.

The lands of silence: a history of Arctic and Antarctic exploration.
See item no. 30.

Eskimos and explorers.
See item no. 34.

The Norse discoveries of America: the Wineland sagas.
See item no. 36.

The Norse Atlantic saga, being the Norse voyages of discovery and settlement to Iceland, Greenland and America.
See item no. 37.

A history of the Vikings.
See item no. 38.

Herdsmen & hermits: Celtic seafarers in the northern seas.
See item no. 39.

Vikings!
See item no. 40.

Viking expansion westwards.
See item no. 41.

The Vinland sagas: the Norse discovery of America. Grænlendinga saga and Eirik's saga.
See item no. 42.

The conquest of the North Atlantic.
See item no. 43.

The European discovery of America. Volume 1: The northern voyages AD 500-1600.
See item no. 44.

In northern mists: Arctic exploration in early times.
See item no. 45.

Northern mists.
See item no. 46.

The heroic age of Scandinavia.
See item no. 48.

The Vikings and their origins: Scandinavia in the first millennium.
See item no. 49.

Arctic exploration.
See item no. 340.

Modern history to the 20th century

189 **Hans Egede, colonizer and missionary of Greenland.**
Louis Bobé.   Copenhagen: Rosenkilde and Bagger, 1952. 207p. map.
A biography of the Danish missionary who led the Danish resettlement of Greenland in the eighteenth century. The book is based on Egede's diaries and reports, public records, and the author's own investigations in Greenland.

190 **A history of the missions in Greenland and Labrador.**
John Carne.   New York: Lane & Tippett, 1848. 218p.
The first part of the book (p. 7-145) relates the story of the missionary work in Greenland by Hans Egede and the Moravian Brethren, giving most attention to the Moravians.

191 **The history of Greenland, including an account of the mission carried on by the United Brethren in that country . . . with a continuation to the present time; illustrative notes; and an appendix, containing a sketch of the Brethren in Labrador.**
David Crantz.   London: Longman, Hurst, Rees, Orme & Brown, 1820.
A history of Greenland and its inhabitants and a description of Moravian missionary activities there. This is a revised and abridged edition of the German edition published in 1767.

192   **A voyage to the Arctic in the whaler Aurora.**
David Moore Lindsay.   Boston: D. Estes, 1911. 223p.
A young surgeon's expanded diary of his experiences on an 1884 whaling voyage tells
of the trials and adventures of hunting and whaling off the east coast of Greenland and
provides some information about the Greenland Eskimos.

193   **Sermermiut in the middle of the nineteenth century.**
Tinna Møbjerg, Kirsten Caning.   *Arctic Anthropology*, vol. 23,
nos. 1-2 (1986), p. 177-98. bibliog.
An interdisciplinary study of a settlement, Sermermiut, in the Disko Bay area which
was abandoned around 1850. Life in the village is described on the basis of evidence
from parish registers and censuses, a traveller's published report, and the excavation of
a Sermermiut house.

194   **The spread of printing – western hemisphere – Greenland.**
Kurt Oldenow, edited by Colin Clair.   Amsterdam: Vangendt;
London: Routledge & Kegan Paul; New York: Abner Schram, 1969.
72p. map.
A history of printing and printers in Greenland, covering the earliest printed book in
1793, the efforts of Hinrich Rink in the 1850s, the publication of the newspaper
Atuagagdliutit in 1861, and the printing of picture books, legends, maps, and official
publications. Essentially the same book as Oldenow's *Printing in Greenland*
(Copenhagen: Munksgaard, 1959, 44p, map), with minor corrections and the inclusion
of illustrations.

195   **Amid Greenland snows or the early history of Arctic missions.**
Jesse Page.   New York; Chicago; Toronto: Fleming H. Revell, [n.d.].
2nd ed. 160p.
An account of Christian missions in Greenland, written in a popular style to display
'the patient and heroic endeavour in the cause of the Cross'. It is concerned principally
with the eighteenth century missionary work of Hans Egede and the Moravian
Brethren but also includes some descriptions of the life and customs of Greenlanders at
that time.

196   **On the variations of settlement pattern and hunting conditions in three
districts of Greenland.**
Robert Petersen.   In: *Circumpolar problems: habitat, economy, and
social relations in the Arctic: a symposium for anthropological research
in the north, September 1969.* Edited by Gösta Berg. Oxford:
Pergamon, 1973, p. 153-61. (Wenner- Gren Center International
Symposium Series, vol. 21).
An examination of population mobility in relation to hunting productivity in the
Upernavik, Ammassalik, and Julianehåb districts of Greenland, primarily in the
nineteenth century.

197   **Greenland: being extracts from a journal kept in that country in the years 1770 to 1778.**
Hans Egede Saabye.   London: Boosey & Sons, 1818. 293p. map.
The author was the grandson of the eighteenth century pioneer missionary to Greenland, Hans Egede. Selections from his journal give insights into Eskimo life and the changes in it brought about by the introduction of Christianity.

198   **Printing in Greenland, with a list of Greenland imprints in the Krabbe Library.**
Nathan Van Patten.   Stanford, California: Stanford University Press, 1939. 40p.
A brief history of the development of printing in Greenland from the use of the first printing press in the late eighteenth century to the 1920s. Included is an annotated list of Greenland imprints in the Krabbe Library at Stanford University.

199   **A collection of documents on Spitzbergen & Greenland.**
Edited by Adam White.   New York: Burt Franklin, [n.d.]. 288p. maps.
The two documents dealing with Greenland are Isaac de la Peyrère's 'History of Greenland' of 1663 (p. 178-249) and Edward Pellham's 'God's power and providence showed in the miraculous preservation and deliverance of eight Englishmen left by mischance in Greenland, anno 1630, nine months and twelve dayes' (p. 251-83). Originally published by the Hakluyt Society (London, 1855).

Safe return doubtful: the heroic age of polar exploration.
See item no. 31.

To the Arctic! the story of northern exploration from earliest times to the present.
See item no. 32.

Eskimos and explorers.
See item no. 34.

Greenland, the adjacent seas, and the North-West Passage to the Pacific Ocean, illustrated in a voyage to Davis's strait during the summer of 1817.
See item no. 63.

To Greenland's icy mountains: the story of Hans Egede, explorer, colonist, missionary.
See item no. 331.

Arctic exploration.
See item no. 340.

20th century

200 Come north with me: an autobiography.
Bernt Balchen.   New York: E. P. Dutton, 1958. 318p. maps.
The life of a pioneer aviator of the Arctic and Antarctic regions, with an account of his wartime adventures in Greenland. During the Second World War he established the ferrying station at Sondre Strømfjord so that military planes could be transferred to Europe.

201 War below zero: the battle for Greenland.
Bernt Balchen, Corey Ford, Oliver La Farge.   Boston: Houghton Mifflin, 1944; London: Allen & Unwin, 1945. 127p.
A popularly-written account of the deeds and adventures of American airmen in Greenland during the Second World War.

202 Americans stand guard in Greenland.
Andrew H. Brown.   *National Geographic Magazine*, vol. 90, no. 4 (October 1946), p. 457-500. map.
An informal chronicle of life on American bases in Greenland, during and just after the Second World War.

203 Lifelines through the Arctic.
William S. Carlson.   New York: Duell, Sloane and Pearce, 1962. 271p. map. bibliog.
The story of American military aviation in the Arctic during and after the Second World War. It includes accounts of the arduous task of building airfields on the edges of the Greenland ice cap in the early days of the war, and of the later development of BMEWS (Ballistic Missile Early Warning System) at Thule in 1960.

204 City under the ice: the story of Camp Century.
Charles Michael Daugherty.   New York: Macmillan; London: Collier-Macmillan, 1963. 156p. maps.
A first-hand account, with many black-and-white photographs, of the facilities and operations of the US Army Polar Research and Development Center's scientific base on the Greenland ice cap, 800 miles from the North Pole.

205 Give me my father's body: the life of Minik, the New York Eskimo.
Kenn Harper.   Frobisher Bay, Northwest Territories: Blacklead Books, 1986. 275p. map. bibliog.
The tragic biography of Minik, an Eskimo from northwestern Greenland, who in 1897 was taken by Admiral Peary to New York where he was adopted by an American family. Upon a visit to the American Museum of Natural History, he suffered the shock of finding his father's skeleton on display. He went back to Greenland in 1909 and had to relearn his native language and the hunting skills he needed for survival. He served as a guide and interpreter for Donald MacMillan's Crocker Land expedition in 1913, returned to the United States in 1916, and died in the influenza epidemic of 1918.

206 **The sledge patrol.**
David Howarth. London: Collins; New York: Macmillan, 1957. 255p.
(233p. in American edition). maps.
The adventures of a small group of Danes and Norwegians assigned to patrol a 500-mile stretch of the northeast Greenland coast during the Second World War and to protect weather stations from German attack.

207 **Hitch your wagon: the story of Bernt Balchen.**
Clayton Knight, Robert C. Durham. Drexel Hill, Pennsylvania: Bell, 1950. 332p. map.
The biography of the famous American aviator whose adventurous life involved supervising the construction of airstrips and directing rescue missions for airmen shot down in Greenland during the Second World War.

208 **The third front: the strange story of the secret war in the Arctic.**
Douglas Liversidge. London: Souvenir, 1960. 219p.
A story of the conflict in the Arctic between the Allies and Germany during the Second World War. Both sides sought to maintain weather stations in Greenland, and the United States Coast Guard and the Danish sledge patrol tried to counter German meteorological activities there.

209 **America, Scandinavia, and the Cold War 1945-1949.**
Geir Lundestad. New York: Columbia University Press, 1980. 434p.
Investigates the relationship between the United States and the Scandinavian countries during the early years of the Cold War. Besides the general discussion, there are specific examinations of American–Danish relations, the Danish decision to join NATO, and the importance of Greenland bases to the United States.

210 **Greenland turns to America.**
James K. Penfield. *National Geographic Magazine*, vol. 82, no. 3 (September 1942), p. 368-83. map.
A description of Greenland in the early years of the American military presence during the Second World War, written by the then American consul at Godthåb.

211 **Greenland: the dispute between Norway and Denmark.**
John Skeie. London, Toronto: J. M. Dent, 1932. 94p. maps.
A Norwegian jurist defends Norway's claims to Greenland in the dispute that was finally settled by the International Court.

212 **The eastern Greenland case in historical perspective.**
Oscar Svarlien. Gainesville, Florida: University of Florida Press, 1964. 74p.
Analyses the territorial dispute between Denmark and Norway and its settlement by the International Court in 1931 in a decision that held Denmark to possess a valid title to sovereignty over all of Greenland.

13 **Economic principles of the Greenland administration before 1947.**
    P. P. Sveistrup.   Copenhagen: Commission for Scientific Investigation
    in Greenland, 1949. 215p. (Reports on Greenland, vol. 150, no. 1).
This work scrutinizes the Greenland economy and examines the controls and pricing
policies imposed by the government monopoly over trade in the years before 1947.

14 **Ice is where you find it.**
    Charles W. Thomas.   Indianapolis, Indiana; New York: Bobbs-
    Merrill, 1951. 378p. maps.
The author, a former Coast Guard officer, relates the story of the 'Greenland Patrol'
and its operations against German attempts to establish meteorological stations along
the east coast of Greenland during the Second World War.

Safe return doubtful: the heroic age of polar exploration.
See item no. 31.

Arctic odyssey: the life of Rear Admiral Donald B. Macmillan.
See item no. 74.

Arctic exploration.
See item no. 340.

Inuit history

215 **Greenlanders and Lapps: some comparisons of their relationship to the
     inclusive society.**
     Vilhelm Aubert.   In: *Circumpolar problems: habitat, economy, and
     social relations in the Arctic: a symposium for anthropological research
     in the north, 5 September 1969*. Edited by Gösta Berg. Oxford:
     Pergamon, 1973, p. 1-8. (Wenner-Gren Center International
     Symposium Series, vol. 21).
Aubert compares the relationships of Greenlanders to Danish society with those of
Lapps to Norwegian society and concludes that Denmark's Greenland policy has been
much more conscious, systematic, and intensive than Norwegian Lappish policy.

216 **Eskimos.**
     Kaj Birket-Smith.   New York: Crown, 1971. 278p. maps. bibliog.
A very useful and well-illustrated introduction to the Greenland Eskimos, from the
discovery and first settlement of the island to the present. Much attention is given to
the Greenlanders' struggle for existence in an inhospitable terrain and to their
language, society, view of life, and relations with the Danes and others. The book first
appeared in Danish in 1927 and then in a revised and enlarged English edition
(London: Methuen, 1936, 1959).

217 **Peoples of the earth: the Arctic.**
Hugh Brody. London: Robert B. Clarke, Danbury, 1973. 144p.
maps. (Peoples of the Earth, vol. 16).

In this volume on the Arctic peoples, three selections focus on Greenland. Jean
Malaurie discusses 'Polar Eskimo – northern Greenland' (p. 86-97); R. Kennedy
Skipton writes of 'West Greenland Eskimo' (p. 98-103); and Robert Gessain examines
'Ammassalmiut – East Greenland' (p. 104-07).

218 **The Eskimos.**
Ernest S. Burch, Jr. Norman, Oklahoma: University of Oklahoma
Press, 1988. 128p. map. bibliog.

An excellent introduction to the world of the Eskimos, this ethnographic study
concentrates on traditional society and explores the Eskimos' art, mythology, beliefs,
and social life. Treated together are the Arctic peoples of Greenland, Alaska, Canada,
and the Soviet Union. More than a hundred colour photographs by Werner Forman
complement the text.

219 **Greenland lies north.**
William S. Carlson. New York: Macmillan, 1940. 306p. maps.

A chronicle of two years' life in Greenland, one year in southern Greenland and the
second in a camp near the northernmost settlements. The author, who lived with an
Eskimo family and observed their way of life, was part of an expedition that studied
winter air currents.

220 **Eskimo diary.**
Thomas Frederiksen, translated by Jack Jensen, Val Clery. London:
Pelham, 1981. 148p. maps.

The life of an Eskimo fishing community is described in a diary kept by a Greenlander
(born 1939) from the early days of his youth. Accompanying reproductions of the diary
are watercolours by the author.

221 **Arctic adventure: my life in the frozen north.**
Peter Freuchen. New York: Farrar & Rinehart, 1935; London:
William Heinemann, 1936. 467p. maps.

An autobiographical account of the author's adventures as an explorer, along with his
detailed observations on life among the Greenland Eskimos. Freuchen's experience
with the Eskimos began in 1906, when he joined a Danish expedition to Greenland,
and continued throughout his life. He lived for a time in Thule and made extensive
travels in the Arctic.

222 **Ice floes and flaming water: a true adventure in Melville Bay.**
Peter Freuchen, translated from the Danish by Johan Hambro. New
York: Julian Messner, 1954. 242p.

An exciting tale of the rescue of a group of whale hunters, stranded by treacherous ice
near Greenland's Melville Bay. The rescuers themselves came close to death several
times, and, faced with bad weather, the group had to seek refuge in a cave or a camp,
consoling themselves by telling stories of their adventures.

223 **The Peter Freuchen reader.**
Peter Freuchen, selected by Dagmar Freuchen. New York: Julian
Messner, 1965. 471p.
A selection of stories and non-fiction pieces by the Danish explorer, mainly about his
travels in the Arctic and his experiences with the people of Greenland.

224 **Peter Freuchen's book of the Eskimo.**
Peter Freuchen, edited by Dagmar Freuchen. Cleveland, New York:
World, 1961; London: Arthur Barker, 1962. 441p. map.
Peter Freuchen's experiences with the Eskimos of Greenland covered more than fifty
years. He lived with them, hunted with them, sang and travelled with them. He was
married for ten years to an Eskimo woman, with whom he had two children. His book
offers a thorough discussion of all aspects of Eskimo life and culture.

225 **Circumpolar peoples: an anthropological perspective.**
Nelson H. H. Graburn, B. Stephen Strong. Pacific Palisades,
California: Goodyear, 1973. 236p. maps. bibliog.
This introduction to the northern peoples of Eurasia and America includes a brief
discussion of the present condition of the Greenland Inuit, within a treatment of Inuit
environment, socioeconomic organization, and religion.

226 **Arctic researches and life among the Esquimaux: being the narrative of
an expedition in search of Sir John Franklin, in the years 1860, 1861,
and 1862.**
Charles Francis Hall. New York: Harper, 1865. 595p. maps.
The author led an American party in a search for the lost Franklin expedition. In the
course of the journey, his ship stopped in Greenland, and Hall provides interesting
descriptions of social conditions there in the mid-nineteenth century, and especially of
the life of the Eskimo.

227 **The snow people.**
Marie Herbert. New York: G. P. Putnam's Sons, 1973. 229p. map.
The story of a year's stay by Marie and Wally Herbert with polar Eskimos in the Thule
district of northwest Greenland. The author learned to skin foxes, to make sealskin
shoes and polar-bear pants, and to share in many of the experiences of the strenuous
yet exhilarating life of the Greenlanders.

228 **Hunters of the polar north: the Eskimos.**
Wally Herbert and the editors of Time-Life Books. Amsterdam:
Time-Life Books, 1981. 168p. maps. bibliog. (Peoples of the Wild).
A book on the Eskimos of northwest Greenland, focusing on the traditional culture
that has endured because of their isolation. Detailed accounts of their way of life are
accompanied by a wealth of colour photographs.

229 **N by E.**
Rockwell Kent. Middletown, Connecticut: Wesleyan University
Press, 1978. 281p.

An account of the artist's voyage with two other men to Greenland in a small boat,
their shipwreck, and their rescue and stay among the Greenlanders. Illustrated by
wood block prints by the author. An appendix includes fourteen Eskimo poems.

230 **Rockwell Kent's Greenland journal: a private diary and sketchbook.**
Rockwell Kent. New York: Ivan Obolensky, 1962. 302p.

The artist's observations and sketches of Eskimo life during a year spent in northern
Greenland in 1931. The diary provided the raw materials for his more finished book,
Salamina (q.v.).

231 **Salamina.**
Rockwell Kent. New York: Harcourt, Brace, 1935. 336p.

The artist tells, in a somewhat romanticized way, of the everyday life of the Greenland
people with whom he stayed for a year. The book, with woodcut illustrations by the
author, is named for the Eskimo housekeeper who ruled him with an iron hand.

232 **Bibliography of bibliographies on the Inuit.**
Inge Kleivan. In: *Arctica 1978: 7th Northern Libraries Colloquy,
19-23 September 1978*. Edited by Sylvie Devers. Paris: Éditions du
Centre National de la Recherche Scientifique, 1982, p. 39-41.

A bibliography of bibliographies (including a listing of other works with extensive
bibliographies) on the Inuit of Greenland and other Arctic regions.

233 **An African in Greenland.**
Tété-Michel Kpomassie, translated from the French by James Kirkup.
New York: Harcourt Brace Jovanovich; London: Martin Secker &
Warburg, 1983. 289p. map.

The author, a young African from Togo, became fascinated with Greenland after
reading a book about Eskimos and finally managed to get there for an extended stay.
French-educated, he observed the Greenland way of life and its traditions and culture
through both French and African eyes, shared in the Greenlanders' experiences, and in
this volume gives a personal, non-scientific account of what he saw and learned.

234 **Oil and amulets: Inuit, a people united at the top of the world.**
Philip Lauritzen, translated by Paula Hostrup-Jessen, Kirsten
Kirkegaard, and Adam Burri. Anchorage, Alaska: Breakwater
Books, 1983. 278p. bibliog. (Arctic and Northern Life Series).

Reviews changes in the life of the Inuit peoples of Greenland, Canada, and Alaska
since the studies of them by Knud Rasmussen, the Danish explorer and anthropologist,
in the 1920s. Inuit delegates to the Circumpolar Conferences express their opinions,
and the text of the Inuit Circumpolar Conference Charter is included. The book was
first published in Denmark with the title *Olie og amuletter* (['Oil and amulets'],
Copenhagen: Informations Forlag, 1979).

235 **The last kings of Thule: a year among the polar Eskimos of Greenland.**
Jean Malaurie, translated from the French by Gwendolen Freeman.
New York: Thomas Y. Crowell, 1956. 295p.

The author, a French geographer, spent 1950 in Greenland, making maps and collecting geological specimens. His book describes everyday life with the polar Eskimos in one of the northernmost settlements in the world.

236 **Eskimo life.**
Fridtjof Nansen, translated by William Archer. London: Longmans, Green, 1894. 2nd ed. 350p.

The famous explorer spent a winter with the Eskimos of West Greenland, hunted with them, shared their life, learned their language, and recorded his observations. The book is full of details about the Eskimos' appearance and dress, kayaks, tents and winter houses, social conditions, food, love and marriage, morals, social organization, religion, art, music, and poetry.

237 **Skinboats of Greenland.**
H. C. Petersen. Roskilde, Denmark: Viking Museum, 1986. 215p.
(Ships and Boats of the North, vol. 1).

A detailed description of how Greenland skinboats – the umiak and the kayak – are built and used. For his information, the author draws upon writings, boats in museums, and his own knowledge as a native Greenlander.

238 **Polar Eskimos of Greenland and their environment.**
William E. Powers. *Journal of Geography*, vol. 49, no. 5 (May 1950), p. 186-93.

A summary of the Greenland Eskimos' traditional way of life and a brief description of the changes occurring as a result of European contacts, trade, and military activities. The author was pessimistic about the Eskimos' future.

239 **The people of the polar north: a record.**
Knud Rasmussen. Compiled from the Danish original and edited by G. Herring. London: Kegan Paul, Trench, Trübner, 1908. 358p. map.

Describes the life, traditions, religion, and folklore of the Greenland Eskimos, especially of the small nomadic group in the northwestern region. It is based on the author's sojourn with them in the winter of 1903-04.

240 **Danish Greenland: its people and products.**
Henrik Rink. Montreal: McGill-Queen's University Press; London: C. Hurst; Copenhagen: Arnold Busck, 1974. 468p.

An account of Greenland in the mid-nineteenth century by a Danish natural scientist and geographer who served for many years in the Greenland administration. This reprint of an 1877 book gives much attention to physical features, climate, and economic resources, as well as discussing the life, beliefs and customs of the Greenlanders and their relations with the Danes.

241 **Anthropological and opthalmological studies on the Angmagssalik Eskimos.**
Erik Skeller.   Copenhagen: Commission for Scientific Investigation in Greenland, 1954. 211p. (Reports on Greenland, vol. 107, no. 4).

An anthropological study of the Eskimos of Ammassalik in southeast Greenland. The work includes a discussion of anthropometrical measurements of Eskimo skeletons, a description of such genetically conditioned characteristics of the Ammassalik as astigmatism, myopia, and colour blindness, and a comparison with other Greenlanders in these respects.

242 **My Eskimo life.**
Paul-Emile Victor, translated from the French by Jocelyn Godefroi.
New York: Simon and Schuster, 1939. 349pp. maps.

The author spent a year at Ammassalik in 1936-37, collecting items for the Museum of Ethnography in Paris. He lived with, and studied, the semi-nomadic Eskimos of the region, learned their language, shared their activities, and describes many aspects of their life.

243 **Saga of a supercargo.**
Fullerton Waldo.   Philadelphia: Macrae Smith, 1926. 309p. map.

A journalist's report on a voyage by tramp steamer from Philadelphia to Greenland that includes descriptions of cryolite mining and Eskimo life.

244 **The Eskimos: their environment and folkways.**
Edward Moffat Weyer.   Hamden, Connecticut: Archon Books, 1969. 491p. maps. bibliog.

Finding a cultural sameness from Alaska to Greenland, the author seeks to portray Eskimo life through its customs and beliefs. Included are discussions of diet and health, the influence of geography and climate, methods of travel, population problems, intertribal relations, social organization, property, the folk traditions of law and order, and religion and taboos. This was published originally by Yale University Press in 1932.

Facts about Denmark.
See item no. 3.

The Arctic.
See item no. 4.

Two summers in Greenland: an artist's adventures among ice and islands, in fjords and mountains.
See item no. 6.

Handbook of North American Indians. Volume 5. Arctic.
See item no. 8.

Some characteristic problems in present-day Greenland.
See item no. 12.

Greenland.
See item no. 23.

Eskimos and explorers.
See item no. 34.

In northern mists: Arctic exploration in early times.
See item no. 45.

An Arctic boat journey, in the autumn of 1854.
See item no. 53.

The land of desolation; being a personal narrative of observation and adventure in Greenland.
See item no. 54.

The first crossing of Greenland.
See item no. 62.

Greenland, the adjacent seas, and the North-West Passage to the Pacific Ocean, illustrated in a voyage to Davis's strait during the summer of 1817.
See item no. 63.

I sailed with Rasmussen.
See item no. 78.

Greenland by the polar sea: the story of the Thule expedition from Melville Bay to cape Morris Jessup.
See item no. 87.

The polar regions: a physical and economic geography of the Arctic and Antarctic.
See item no. 99.

Geography of the northlands.
See item no. 104.

The Poles.
See item no. 106.

An historical and descriptive account of Iceland, Greenland and the Faroe Islands, with illustrations of their natural history.
See item no. 108.

The geography of the polar regions consisting of a general characterization of polar nature by Otto Nordenskjöld and a regional geography of the Arctic and the Antarctic by Ludwig Mecking.
See item no. 109.

Problems of polar research: a series of papers by thirty-one authors.
See item no. 111.

The Arctic basin.
See item no. 112.

To the Arctic: an introduction to the far northern world.
See item no. 117.

Polar regions atlas.
See item no. 121.

Greenland icefields and life in the North Atlantic, with a new discussion of the causes of the Ice Age.
See item no. 138.

The history of Greenland. Vol. I. Earliest times to 1700. Vol. II. 1700-1782. Vol. III. 1782-1808.
See item no. 179.

A voyage to the Arctic in the whaler Aurora.
See item no. 192.

Greenland: being extracts from a journal kept in that country in the years 1770 to 1778.
See item no. 197.

Under four flags: recent cultural change among the Eskimos.
See item no. 261.

The fourth world: the heritage of the Arctic and its destruction.
See item no. 286.

What the Greenlanders want.
See item no. 288.

'It's too bad you're Greenlanders'.
See item no. 289.

Tales and traditions of the Eskimo.
See item no. 320.

Eskimos.
See item no. 326.

Eskimos of the world.
See item no. 328.

Eskimos.
See item no. 333.

Eskimos.
See item no. 338.

Iceland and Greenland.
See item no. 343.

The Indians and Eskimos of North America: a bibliography of books in print through 1972.
See item no. 371.

Ethnographic bibliography of North America.
See item no. 373.

Language

245 **Eskimo languages: their present-day conditions: 'Majority language influence on Eskimo minority languages'.**
Edited by Bjarne Basse, Kirsten Jensen. Aarhus, Denmark: Arkona, 1979. 200p. bibliog.

A collection of papers from a symposium in the Department of Greenlandic at Aarhus University in 1978. Papers on Greenland include: 'What conditions does the Danish state provide for the existence and development of the Greenlandic language?' by Chr. Berthelsen (p. 11-20); 'Danish influence on Greenlandic syntax' by Robert Petersen (p. 113-22); 'Language and the church in Greenland' by Inge Kleivan (p. 123-44); 'Language and identity in Thule' by Regitze Margrethe Søby (p. 145-54); 'The status of the Greenlandic language in Greenland today' by Carl Chr. Olsen (p. 161-66); 'On the adaptation of Danish Christian names to pronunciation habits of the Greenlandic language,' by Jørgen Rischel (p. 167-74); 'Studies in the vocabulary of Greenlandic translations of the Bible' by Inge Kleivan (p. 175-90); and 'Copenhagen Greenlandic' by Robert Petersen (p. 191-96).

246 **What dialect distribution can tell us of dialect formation in Greenland.**
Michael Fortescue. *Arctic Anthropology*, vol. 23, nos. 1-2 (1986), p. 413-22. bibliog.

The author presents a brief account of linguistic papers presented at a 1981 symposium and hypothesizes about dialect formation in Greenland.

247 **Stylistic forms in Greenland Eskimo literature.**
Svend Frederiksen. Copenhagen: Commission for Scientific Investigation in Greenland, 1954. 40p. (Reports on Greenland, vol. 136, no. 7).

An analysis of the Greenland Eskimo language that examines the parts of speech, the functions of nouns and verbs, the coinage of new expressions, and the figures of speech that are used.

248 **Alaska native languages: a bibliographical catalogue. Part one: Indian languages.**
Michael E. Krauss, Mary Jane McGary. Fairbanks, Alaska: University of Alaska, Alaska Native Language Center, 1980. 455p.
Although this bibliography's central focus is the native languages of Alaska, it includes a section on the Eskimos of Greenland.

249 **Eskimo grammar.**
E. J. Peck. Ottawa: Department of the Interior, North West Territories and Yukon Branch, 1931. 92p.
A basic grammar, originally published in 1919, of the Inuit language, with a guide to pronunciation. The author drew upon Kleinschmidt's grammar of Greenlandic and upon translations by the Moravian Brethren, as well as on his six years of residence in the Canadian north.

250 **Some features common to East and West Greenlandic in the light of dialect relationships and the latest migration theories.**
Robert Petersen. *Arctic Anthropology*, vol. 23, nos. 1-2 (1986), p. 401-11. bibliog.
The East Greenlandic and West Greenlandic dialects appear different, but the underlying structure indicates a common origin. Based on dialect studies, new theories on migration within Greenland are developed.

251 **Tunumiit oraasiat: the East Greenlandic Inuit language.**
P. Robbé, Louis-Jacques Dorais. Quebec: Université Laval, 1986. 265p. (Collection Nordicana, 49).
A grammar and dictionary of the East Greenland language, with translations in Danish, English, French, and West Greenlandic.

252 **Dictionary of the West Greenlandic Eskimo language.**
C. W. Schultz-Lorentzen. Copenhagen: C. A. Reitzel, 1927. 303p.
West Greenlandic is the official language of Greenland. This dictionary provides a listing of some of the most common words and includes phonetic guides. This originally appeared in *Meddelseler om Grønland*, vol. 69. (q.v.).

253 **A grammar of the West Greenland language.**
Christian Wilhelm Schultz-Lorentzen. Copenhagen: Commission for Scientific Investigation in Greenland, 1945. 104p. (Reports on Greenland, vol. 129, no. 3).
Based on the pioneering research of Samuel Kleinschmidth and W. Thalbitzer, this concise grammar of the West Greenland language was especially designed for use by teachers.

Handbook of North American Indians. Volume 5. Arctic.
See item no. 8.

Language

Greenland: past and present.
See item no. 14.

Eskimos.
See item no. 216.

The polar Eskimos: language and folklore.
See item no. 317.

Religion

254 **The revival at Pisugfik in 1768: an ethnohistorical approach.**
Hans Christian Gulløv. *Arctic Anthropology*, vol. 23, nos. 1-2 (1986), p. 151-75. bibliog.
An account of a revival in an Eskimo settlement north of Godthåb in 1768. A shaman who had a dream of belief in Jesus led his relatives to the European settlements for baptism. The author examines this event in the light of historical documents, oral traditions, and archaeological observations.

255 **The Danish Church.**
Edited by Poul Hartling, translated from the Danish by Sigurd Mammen. Copenhagen: Danish Institute (Det Danske Selskab), 1965. 161p.
Explains many aspects of the Danish national church (Evangelical Lutheran) as it exists in Denmark, Greenland, and the Faroes: its service, architecture, history, organization and government, and activities.

256 **Eskimos, Greenland and Canada.**
I. Kleivan, B. Sonne. Leiden, Netherlands: E. J. Brill, 1985. 43p. map. bibliog. (Iconography of Religions, 8).
A description of the Eskimo religion, with information on rites of passage in the individual's life cycle, hunting rituals, ritual behaviour in social conflict, the role of the shaman, and the various deities. Illustrated by forty-eight black-and-white plates of drawings and photographs. This is part of a series published by the Institute of Religious Iconography, University of Groningen in the Netherlands.

Religion

257 **Toornaarsuk, an historical Proteus.**
Birgitte Sonne. *Arctic Anthropology*, vol. 23, nos. 1-2 (1986), p. 199-219. bibliog.

An interpretation of Toornaarsuk, a helping spirit in the Inuit religion who has been viewed both as the worst Evil and the highest Good.

Facts about Denmark.
See item no. 3.

Greenland: past and present.
See item no. 14.

Greenland.
See item no. 23.

Circumpolar peoples: an anthropological perspective.
See item no. 225.

Eskimo life.
See item no. 236.

The people of the polar north: a record.
See item no. 239.

The Eskimos: their environment and folkways.
See item no. 244.

Eskimo languages: their present-day conditions: 'Majority language influence on Eskimo minority languages'.
See item no. 245.

Eskimos.
See item no. 326.

Dance masks of Ammassalik (east coast of Greenland).
See item no. 346.

Society

Social conditions and problems

258 **Urbanization, industrialization and changes in the family in Greenland during the reform period since 1950.**
Agnete Weis Bentzon, Torben Agersnap. In: *Circumpolar problems: habitat, economy, and social relations in the Arctic: a symposium for anthropological research in the north, September 1969.* Edited by Gösta Berg. Oxford: Pergamon, 1973, p. 21-28. bibliog. (Wenner-Gren Center International Symposium Series, vol. 21).
Concomitantly with Denmark's policy of social and economic reforms in Greenland came a marked increase in town population. Economic and technical development in the towns was so rapid that it encouraged family members to remain in an extended household for economic advantages. These research findings apparently contradict the social anthropological theory that urbanization and industrialization are accompanied by vanishing extended family patterns and a transition to the nuclear family pattern.

259 **Territorial rights in Greenland: some preliminary notes.**
Jens Brøsted. *Arctic Anthropology*, vol. 23, nos. 1-2 (1986), p. 325-38. map. bibliog.
An examination of the Greenlandic Inuit system of land tenure, with a brief consideration of the Land Use and Planning Act for Greenland.

260 **The hot Arctic.**
John Dyson. Boston, Massachusetts; Toronto: Little Brown, 1979. 290p. map.
The author sees the Arctic as 'hot' because modernization is bringing its peoples into the contemporary world. He discusses the Greenlanders' social problems: alcoholism, venereal disease, the break-up of the family, unemployment. Dyson believes the

Danes have brought Greenlanders to a stage of 'vigorous but restrained political activity'.

261 **Under four flags: recent culture change among the Eskimos.**
Charles Campbell Hughes. *Current Anthropology*, vol. 6, no.1 (February 1965), p. 3-69. map. bibliog.
An overview of cultural changes among the Eskimos of Greenland, Canada, Alaska, and Siberia. In the section on Greenland (p. 5-12), the author examines the historical and ecological setting for contemporary changes, recent economic development, settlement patterns and community life, the maintenance of traditions, and the changes affecting both the Ammassalik and the Thule Eskimos.

262 **Modernization and traditional interpersonal relations in a small Greenlandic community: a case study from southern Greenland.**
Per Langgaard. *Arctic Anthropology*, vol. 23, nos. 1-2 (1986), p. 299-314. bibliog.
Examines patterns of interpersonal relations and features of social organization in a small village and argues that a radical restructuring may be necessary for survival of the attractive aspects of traditional village life.

263 **Alcohol problems in Greenland.**
Inge Lynge. In: *Symposium on psychiatric epidemiology and suicidology among children and adults in the far north.* Oulu, Finland: Nordic Council for Arctic Medical Research, 1981, p. 71-75. (Nordic Council for Arctic Medical Research report 27/80).
Discusses the problem of increased alcohol consumption in Greenland since the ending of import restrictions in 1950, and examines the measures of control, including the system of rationing adopted in 1979.

264 **Suicide in Greenland.**
Inge Lynge. In: *Symposium on psychiatric epidemiology and suicidology among children and adults in the far north.* Oulu, Finland: Nordic Council for Arctic Medical Research, 1981, p. 88–92. (Nordic Council for Arctic Medical Research report 27/80).
Finds that the suicide rate in Greenland, minimal at the beginning of the twentieth century, has been rapidly increasing. The author relates this alarming acceleration to the socio-cultural changes that have occurred.

265 **Social welfare in Denmark.**
Ernst Marcussen, translated from the Danish by Geoffrey French. Copenhagen: Danish Institute (Det Danske Selskab), 1980. 4th rev. ed. 184p.
An explanation of the social welfare systems of Denmark, Greenland, and the Faroe Islands.

266 **The impact of public planning on ethnic culture: aspects of Danish resettlement policies in Greenland after World War II.**
Marie-Louise Deth Petersen. *Arctic Anthropology*, vol. 23, nos. 1-2 (1986), p. 271-80. bibliog.
This article shows the divergence between social planning and the actual development of housing and resettlement in the postwar years, and indicates how housing development influenced family patterns and the adaptation of households to urban environments.

267 **Forty years of cultural change among the Inuit in Alaska, Canada and Greenland: some reflections.**
Marianne Stenbaek. *Arctic*, vol. 40, no. 4 (December 1987), p. 300-09. bibliog.
The traditional life style of the Arctic peoples has been dramatically altered by the increased influx of southern peoples with their modern technology, bureaucracy, and different economic, political, and social systems. The changes have resulted in much human tragedy, such as suicide epidemics and alcoholism, but they have also brought many positive changes so that Inuit culture is being reaffirmed, the author concludes.

Facts about Denmark.
See item no. 3.

North, Central and South America: Atlantic Islands.
See item no. 11.

The Arctic basin.
See item no. 112.

Polar Eskimos of Greenland and their environment.
See item no. 238.

The Eskimos: their environment and folkways.
See item no. 244.

Criminal homicide in Greenland.
See item no. 275.

Greenland in figures.
See item no. 308.

Health

268 **Greenland medical bibliography.**
Soren Andersen. Oulu, Finland: Nordic Council for Arctic Medical Research, 1981. 137p. (Report 29/81).

A non-annotated bibliography of nearly 5,000 items on health conditions in Greenland from the early days of Hans Egede in the eighteenth century to the 1970s. The compiler was medical officer of the Ammassalik district in Greenland.

269 **Exposure to heavy metals in Greenland from natural and man-made sources.**
Jens C. Hansen. In: *Arctic air pollution*. Edited by Bernard Stonehouse. Cambridge: Cambridge University Press, 1986, p. 249-57. (Studies in Polar Research).

Samples of blood and hair taken from Inuit in Greenland since 1979 have been used to evaluate exposure to mercury, lead, calcium, and selenium. Comparisons with fifteenth century hair show increases in mercury and lead and decreases in selenium. Present exposure levels may be of risk to foetal development, and legal regulations should be considered to protect the Inuit population from the adverse effects of marine and atmospheric pollution.

270 **The Greenland aerosol: elemental composition, seasonal variations and likely sources.**
Niels Z. Heidam. In: *Arctic air pollution*. Edited by Bernard Stonehouse. Cambridge: Cambridge University Press, 1986, p.37-52. (Studies in Polar Research).

Danish research into airborne particles and gases over Greenland finds that the dominant element in the Arctic haze is a combustion component originating from fossil fuel combustion, mainly from industry in the Ural region of the USSR.

271 **Alcohol problems in western Greenland.**
Inge Lynge. In: *Circumpolar Health: proceedings of the 3rd international symposium, Yellowknife, NWT*. Edited by Roy J. Shephard and S. Itoh. Toronto: University of Toronto Press, 1976, p. 543-48.

A brief paper reporting the findings of a medical survey of alcoholism in West Greenland.

272 **Circumpolar health: proceedings of the 3rd international symposium, Yellowknife, NWT.**
Edited by Roy J. Shephard and S. Itoh. Toronto: University of Toronto Press, 1976. 678p.

Among the numerous short papers in this collection are a few on Greenland topics, including current trends of medical research, dietary habits of school children, genetic trends in the population, and housing and sickness in South Greenland.

Greenland.
See item no. 23.

Changing Greenland.
See item no. 181.

Anthropological and opthalmological studies on the Angmagssalik Eskimos.
See item no. 241.

The Eskimos: their environment and folkways.
See item no. 244.

The hot Arctic.
See item no. 260.

Alcohol problems in Greenland.
See item no. 263.

Forty years of cultural change among the Inuit in Alaska, Canada, and Greenland: some reflections.
See item no. 267.

Greenland in figures.
See item no. 308.

Education

273　**The pedagogical situation in Greenland.**
　　　Bent Gunther.　In: *Education in the north: selected papers of the first international conference on cross-cultural education in the circumpolar nations and related articles.* Edited by Frank Darnell. Fairbanks, Alaska: University of Alaska, Arctic Institute of North America, 1972, p. 242-67.
A review of the policies and problems of education in Greenland as of the early 1970s.

274　**Eskimo education, Danish and Canadian: a comparison.**
　　　C. W. Hobart, C. S. Brent.　*Canadian Review of Sociology and Anthropology*, vol. 3, no. 2 (May 1966), p. 47-66.
A comparison, in terms of histories and cultural dynamics, of the systems of Eskimo education in Greenland and the Canadian Arctic. Concludes that the Danish approach to education in Greenland has greatly accelerated the transition to a cultural synthesis, with accompanying disruptive effects, while the magnitude of change in Canada has been much less.

Facts about Denmark.
See item no. 3.

Greenland: past and present.
See item no. 14.

Greenland.
See item no. 23.

Greenland.
See item no. 24.

Greenland and the nature of its administrative arrangements.
See item no. 279.

Economic development in Greenland and its relationship to education.
See item no. 302.

Arctic.
See item no. 364.

Arctic bibliography.
See item no. 375.

Crime

275 **Criminal homicide in Greenland.**
J. P. Hart Hansen. In: *Circumpolar health: proceedings of the 3rd international symposium, Yellowknife, NWT*. Edited by Roy J. Shephard and S. Itoh. Toronto; Buffalo, New York: University of Toronto Press, 1976, p. 548-54.

This study compares the increased frequency of criminal homicide in Greenland since the Second World War with other North Atlantic countries. The increase is explained by an explosive social development with resettlement, profound changes in living conditions, social instability, and increasing abuse of alcohol.

276 **The penal system of Denmark.**
Arne Lönberg. Copenhagen: Ministry of Justice, Department of Prison and Probation, 1975. 3rd ed. 116p. map.

Basic information on the administration of justice in Denmark (the criminal courts, prosecution, criminal investigation and custody, social enquiry reports and mental examinations), the criminal law and its sanctions, the range of possible sentences, parole and pardon, probation, penal institutions, and the organization, staff, and budget of the prison and probation administration. A separate chapter covers these rules and processes in Greenland and the Faroe Islands.

The Eskimos: their environment and folkways.
See item no. 244.

The Greenland criminal code.
See item no. 283.

The Greenland criminal code and its sociological background.
See item no. 284.

Government and Politics

277 **The Nordic parliaments: a comparative analysis.**
David Arter. New York: St. Martin's, 1984. 421p.
Provides descriptions, analyses, and comparisons of the role of the Nordic parliaments (including the Danish Folketing, the Landsting of Greenland, and the Lagting of the Faroe Islands) in the policy-making process. The book provides an almost encyclopedic discussion of legislative structures and procedures in Northern Europe, but the lack of a bibliography is a weakness.

278 **Constitutions of the countries of the world.**
Edited by Albert P. Blaustein, Gisbert H. Flanz. Dobbs Ferry, New York: Oceana Publications, 1986. 17 vols. plus 2 supplements. bibliog.
In volume four (p. 1-99) are the texts of the Danish constitution of 1953 and the Succession to the Throne Act of 1953, the Greenland Home Rule Act of 1978 and a resumé of the Report of the Commission on Home Rule in Greenland, and the Home Rule Act of 1948 for the Faroe Islands. In addition, there are brief summaries of constitutional history and chronology, that for Denmark by Kenneth E. Miller and those for Greenland and the Faroes by Roxann E. Henry and Kenneth E. Miller.

279 **Greenland and the nature of its administrative arrangements.**
N. O. Christensen. In: *Education in the north: selected papers of the first international conference on cross-cultural education in the circumpolar nations and related articles*. Edited by Frank Darnell. Fairbanks, Alaska: University of Alaska, Arctic Institute of North America, 1972, p. 112-21.
A summary of government, administration, and education in Greenland in the time before the establishment of Home Rule in 1979.

280 **Past and contemporary administrative problems in Greenland.**
N. O. Christensen. In: *Arctica 1978: 7th Northern Libraries Colloquy,
19-23 September 1978.* Edited by Sylvie Devers. Paris: Éditions du
Centre National de la Recherche Scientifique, 1982, p. 120-22.

A bibliography of sources in Danish, English, and other languages on the government
and administration of Greenland.

281 **Greenland: political structure of self-government.**
Jens Dahl. *Arctic Anthropology*, vol. 23, nos. 1-2 (1986), p. 315-24.
bibliog.

A discussion of Home Rule in Greenland, covering the structure of government,
politics, the development policies that have been adopted, the radicalization of the
Greenland élite, and an assessment of the benefits and problems of home rule.

282 **Home rule in Greenland.**
Isi Foighel. Copenhagen: Commission for Scientific Research in
Greenland, 1980. 21p.

Includes a copy of the Home Rule Act of 1978 and a discussion of the political events
leading to its adoption. This appeared in *Meddelelser om Grønland: Man and Society*
no. 1.

283 **The Greenland criminal code.**
Translated from the Danish by George Stürup, Johannes Andenaes.
South Hackensack, New Jersey: Fred B. Rothman; London: Sweet &
Maxwell, 1970. 47p.

The text of the Greenland criminal code of 1954. In an introduction, Professor Verner
Goldschmidt, the code's drafter, points out that the code is 'unique in its creation of
sanctions which are inspired, not by the gravity of the offense itself, but by a desire to
rehabilitate the offender and to protect society'. Sanctions are tailored to the individual
in a humanitarian way.

284 **The Greenland criminal code and its sociological background.**
Verner Goldschmidt. *Acta Sociologica*, vol. 1 (1955), p. 256- 65.

A discussion of the development of the 1954 Greenland criminal code, including a
history of the legal norms related to it, by the code's drafter. Also provided is an
English translation of the text of the code.

285 **Peripheries and nationalism: the Faroes and Greenland.**
Olafur Ragnar Grímsson. *Scandinavian Political Studies*, vol. 1 (new
series), no. 4 (1978), p. 315-27.

Suggests a research plan for investigating the political and socioeconomic processes
that create nationalist politics in peripheral regions such as Greenland and the Faroe
Islands.

286 **The fourth world: the heritage of the Arctic and its destruction.**
Sam Hall. New York: Random House; London: The Bodley Head, 1987. 240p. maps. bibliog.
A journalist's account of threats to the Arctic environment and its peoples from hydroelectric plants, oil pipelines and offshore rigs, Western consumer goods, and political and military competition. In Greenland, he sees the resident Danes as 'a privileged class from whose dominance the native Inuit cannot escape' but has some hopes from home rule and the new programmes adopted by the Greenlanders.

287 **Eskimo administration: IV. Greenland.**
Diamond Jenness. Montreal: Arctic Institute of North America, 1967. 176p. maps. bibliog. (AINA Technical Paper no. 19).
A detailed account of Denmark's administration of Greenland from 1721 to the 1960s that examines Danish policies and the political, social, and economic development of the island.

288 **What the Greenlanders want.**
Finn Lynge. *Scandinavian Review*, vol. 71, no. 2 (June 1983), p. 17-27.
Greenland's representative to the European Parliament discusses the goals and interests of Greenlanders and calls on other nations to address the major concerns of Arctic policy: the law of the sea, fish and game in the Arctic, improved communications, cultural policies for aboriginal Arctic peoples and security in the Northern region.

289 **It's too bad you're Greenlanders.**
Karen Nørregaard. *Scandinavian Review*, vol. 66, no. 1 (March 1978), p. 38-43.
Explains the discontent of Greenlanders with Danish rule and the growth of the movement for more home rule.

290 **Greenland: the politics of a new northern nation.**
Nils Ørvik. *International Journal*, vol. 39, no. 4 (Autumn 1984), p. 932-61.
The author discusses the Greenlandic political parties and the nature of their competition, and concludes that the first five years of self-government proved that Greenlanders are 'up to the mark of Western political performance', (p. 961). They have not yet fully appreciated the harsh realities stemming from Greenland's strategic significance, however.

Facts about Denmark.
See item no. 3.

Greenland.
See item no. 5.

North, Central and South America: Atlantic Islands.
See item no. 11.

Greenland: past and present.
See item no. 14.

Greenland: a part of Denmark.
See item no. 16.

Greenland.
See item no. 24.

The land of desolation; being a personal narrative of observation and adventure in Greenland.
See item no. 54.

The circumpolar north: a political and economic geography of the Arctic and sub-Arctic.
See item no. 96.

Geography of the northlands.
See item no. 104.

Changing Greenland.
See item no. 181.

Greenlanders and Lapps: some comparisons of their relationship to the inclusive society.
See item no. 215.

The Eskimos: their environment and folkways.
See item no. 244.

Territorial rights in Greenland: some preliminary notes.
See item no. 259.

The penal system of Denmark.
See item no. 276.

Greenland in figures.
See item no. 308.

Arctic bibliography.
See item no. 375.

Foreign Relations

291   **The United States defence areas in Greenland.**
Clive Archer.   *Cooperation and Conflict*, vol. 23, no. 3 (1988), p. 123-
44.

An examination of the American military presence in Greenland, seen in the context
of broader US strategy. The author points to the effects of the American connection
on Greenland and Denmark and suggests that the 1980s have brought a questioning of
the American defence areas by Greenlandic and Danish politicians.

292   **Greenland and the Arctic region: resources and security policy.**
H. C. Bach, Jørgen Taagholt.   Copenhagen: Information and Welfare
Service of the Danish Defence, 1982. 2nd ed. 79p. maps. bibliog.

Assesses Greenland's natural resources and the island's place in global military
strategy.

293   **Greenland's international fisheries relations: a coastal state in the
'north' with problems of the 'south'?**
Brit Fløistad.   *Cooperation and Conflict*, vol. 24, no. 1 (1989), p. 5-48.

Concludes that with its exit from the European Community, Greenland's need for
financial aid from the EC puts the island in a situation comparable to that of coastal
states in the Third World: it must sell its maritime resources today in order to develop
its national fisheries tomorrow.

294   **Greenland between might and right.**
Harald Flor.   *Scandinavian Review*, vol. 74, no. 2 (Summer 1986),
p. 13-18.

Discusses American military installations in Greenland and the various issues raised by
their presence.

295 **Greenland's withdrawal from the European Communities.**
Frank Harhoff. *Common Market Law Review*, vol. 20, no. 1 (March 1983), p. 13-33.
An explanation of Greenland's 1982 decision to leave the European Communities and a consideration of the problems created for the EC.

296 **The Soviet Union in Arctic waters: security implications for the northern flank of NATO.**
Willy Østreng, translated from Norwegian by Eric Hansen. Honolulu: Law of the Sea Institute, William S. Richardson School of Law, University of Hawaii, 1987. 77p. maps.
An analysis of Soviet naval strategy in the Arctic Ocean, including its significance for the Greenland Sea and the Denmark Strait, east of Greenland. Originally published in Norwegian by Gyldendal Norsk Forlag, 1982.

297 **Denmark, Greenland, and Arctic security.**
Nikolaj Petersen. In: *The Arctic challenge: Nordic and Canadian approaches to security and cooperation in an emerging international region.* Edited by Karl Möttölä. Boulder, Colorado: Westview, 1988. p. 37-73.
A review of Greenland's strategic significance, its contributions to Western defence, and the relation of Greenlandic politics to security questions. The author believes the United States must continue to bear the main responsibility for Greenland's defence.

298 **Soviet strategic interest in maritime Arctic.**
Gerald E. Synhorst. *United States Naval Institute Proceedings*, vol. 99, no. 843 (May 1973), p. 88-111. maps.
Discusses Soviet claims and strategic interests in the Arctic Ocean, including the important passage to the Atlantic known as the Greenland–Iceland–United Kingdom Gap.

299 **Cold water politics: the maritime strategy and geopolitics of the northern front.**
Ola Tunander. London: Sage; Oslo: International Peace Research Institute, PRIO, 1989. 194p. maps. bibliog.
A book on the geopolitics of northern Europe and the northern seas. Several of the possible scenarios for military action involve the Greenland Sea, the waters northeast of Greenland.

300 **US Arctic interests: the 1980s and 1990s.**
Edited by William E. Westermeyer and Kurt M. Shusterich. New York:Springer-Verlag, 1984. 369p. maps.
A collection of papers by natural and social scientists, government officials, and oil industry representatives, most useful as an overall examination of America's strategic and economic interests in the Arctic but including a brief discussion of Greenland's strategic importance.

Facts about Denmark.
See item no. 3.

Handbook of North American Indians. Volume 5. Arctic.
See item no. 8.

Greenland: a part of Denmark.
See item no. 16.

Greenland.
See item no. 24.

The circumpolar north: a political and economic geography of the Arctic and sub-Arctic.
See item no. 96.

Geography of the northlands.
See item no. 104.

Arctic geology: proceedings of the second international symposium on Arctic geology, held February 1-4, 1971, at San Francisco, California.
See item no. 135.

Changing Greenland.
See item no. 181.

America, Scandinavia, and the Cold War 1945-1949.
See item no. 209.

Greenland: the dispute between Norway and Denmark.
See item no. 211.

The eastern Greenland case in historical perspective.
See item no. 212.

What the Greenlanders want.
See item no. 288.

Greenland: the politics of a new northern nation.
See item no. 290.

Economy

301 Sheep rearing in South Greenland: an analysis of the present-day problems of adaptation.
Hans Berg. In: *Circumpolar problems: habitat, economy, and social relations in the Arctic: a symposium for anthropological research in the north, September 1969.* Edited by Gösta Berg. Oxford: Pergamon, 1973, p. 29-37. (Wenner-Gren Center International Symposium Series, vol. 21).
An attempt to explain the adaptive changes in the sheep industry in South Greenland. The author looks at sheep-raising both in terms of the individual household and in its relation to the larger society and suggests that producers' cooperatives would be an alternative to the present organization of the industry.

302 Economic development in Greenland and its relationship to education.
Claus Bornemann. In: *Education in the north: selected papers of the first international conference on cross-cultural education in the circumpolar nations and related articles.* Edited by Frank Darnell. Fairbanks, Alaska: University of Alaska, Arctic Institute of North America, 1972, p. 212-26.
An analysis of Greenland's economic situation in the early 1970s. Despite its title, the article has little to say about education.

303 Greenland – its economy and resources.
Lise Lyck, Jørgen Taagholt. *Arctic*, vol. 40, no. 1 (March 1987), p. 50-59. bibliog.
This describes the development of Greenland toward greater autonomy and examines the economy, minerals, and energy resources. The economy is characterized as small, mixed, and vulnerable, with considerable inflation, the beginnings of unemployment

problems, and extreme dependence on capital inflow and skilled labour from Denmark.

304 **Petroleum potential in Arctic North America and Greenland.**
Walter W. Nassichuk. In: *Arctic energy resources: proceedings of the Comité Arcticque international conference on Arctic energy resources held at the Veritas Centre, Oslo, Norway, September 22-24, 1982.* Edited by Louis Rey. Amsterdam: Elsevier, 1983, p. 51-88. (Energy Research, vol. 2).
Concludes that the Wandel Sea Basin of northeastern Greenland has excellent hydrocarbon potential. The cost of recovering petroleum may be very high, however, and drilling in a region of shifting ice presents serious problems.

305 **Recording the utilization of land and sea resources in Greenland.**
H. C. Petersen. *Arctic Anthropology*, vol. 23, nos. 1-2 (1986), p. 259-69. map. bibliog.
Discussed here is the author's work in recording human and animal use of land and sea areas in West Greenland. Such information is helpful in showing changes in the ecological balance.

306 **Kap Hope: a settlement and its resources.**
Hanne Sandell, Birger Sandell. *Arctic Anthropology*, vol. 23, nos. 1-2 (1986), p. 281-98. map. bibliog.
A study of the settlement of Kap Hope in northeastern Greenland, founded in 1925. The article shows an economy that remains based on hunting and that has adopted modern technology to utilize the region's resources in a traditional way.

307 **The Arctic resources' possible part in future energy politics.**
Jørgen Taagholt. In: *European security, nuclear weapons and public confidence.* Edited by William Gutteridge, Marian Dobrosielski, Jorma Miettinen. London; Basingstoke, England; Macmillan; New York: St. Martin's,1982. p. 155-67.
This argues that the use of raw materials and energy resources in relatively inaccessible Arctic areas may soon become reality despite the high investment required. The resources in Greenland include coal, uranium, oil and gas, and hydroelectric power.

Facts about Denmark.
See item no. 3.

Greenland.
See item no. 5.

North, Central and South America: Atlantic islands.
See item no. 11.

Some characteristic problems in present-day Greenland.
See item no. 12.

Greenland: past and present.
See item no. 14.

Greenland: a part of Denmark.
See item no. 16.

Greenland.
See item no. 24.

The circumpolar north: a political and economic geography of the Arctic and sub-Arctic.
See item no. 96.

Geography of the northlands.
See item no. 104.

The Scandinavian world.
See item no. 110.

Polar regions atlas.
See item no. 121.

Changing Greenland.
See item no. 181.

Economic principles of the Greenland administration before 1947.
See item no. 213.

Under four flags: recent culture change among the Eskimos.
See item no. 261.

Greenland in figures.
See item no. 308.

Iceland and Greenland.
See item no. 343.

Statistics

308   **Greenland in figures.**
Copenhagen: Prime Minister's Office, Greenland Department, 1987.
45p.
A brief compendium of basic statistics on Greenland, including figures on population, employment, public finance, imports and exports, wages and prices, transport, housing conditions, social welfare, hospitals and health, education, and elections.

309   **Grønland. Årsberetning.** (Annual Report.)
Copenhagen: Ministry for Greenland. annual.
An official yearbook, in Danish with English translations of statistical tables.

310   **Statistisk Årbog.** (Statistical Yearbook.)
Copenhagen: Danmarks Statistik og Socialforskningsinstituttet. annual.
A comprehensive statistical description of Denmark, Greenland, and the Faroe Islands, with subheadings and index in English. An extensive bibliography of other Danish statistical publications is included.

311   **Yearbook of Nordic Statistics/Nordisk Statistisk Årsbok.**
Stockholm: Norstedt, for the Nordic Council. annual.
Basic statistical data on the five Nordic countries, with Greenland included along with Denmark. It is arranged so as to facilitate comparisons. Text and table headings are in both English and Swedish.

Literature

Literary history and criticism

312 **Greenlandic literature: its traditions, changes, and trends.**
Christian Berthelsen. *Arctic Anthropology*, vol. 23, nos. 1-2 (1986),
p. 339-45. bibliog.
Considers the origins of Greenlandic written literature and its development into
modern poetry and prose, and shows the effects of European influences on modern
Greenlandic literature.

313 **A pageant of old Scandinavia.**
Edited by Henry Goddard Leach. Princeton, New Jersey: Princeton
University Press, 1946. 350p. bibliog.
This anthology of old Scandinavian literature has translations from the sagas and the
eddas and includes a chapter on the literature of Greenland to the fourteenth century
(p. 277-81).

Handbook of North American Indians. Volume 5. Arctic.
See item no. 8.

Greenland: past and present.
See item no. 14.

The Norse discoveries of America: the Wineland sagas.
See item no. 36.

**The Vinland sagas: the Norse discovery of America. Grænlendinga saga and
Eirik's saga.**
See item no. 42.

Eskimo life.
See item no. 236.

Fiction, folktales and poetry

314 **The Greenlander.**
Mark Adlard. New York: Summit Books, 1978. 319p.
A novel of adventure, centring on a whaling voyage to the Greenland Sea in the nineteenth century.

315 **Modern Scandinavian poetry (1900-1975).**
Edited by Martin Allwood. New York: New Directions; Mullsjö, Sweden:Anglo-American Centre, 1982. 399p.
An anthology of twentieth century poetry from Denmark (including Greenland and the Faroes) and the other Nordic countries, with brief critical introductions to the poetry of each nation.

316 **Anerca.**
Edited by Edmund Carpenter. Toronto; Vancouver: J. M. Dent, 1959. [n.p.].
A brief collection of Eskimo poems from Greenland and Canada, including hunters' chants, judicial drum-songs, and incantations. In the Eskimo language, 'anerca' means the soul.

317 **The polar Eskimo: language and folklore.**
Eric Holtved. Copenhagen: Commission for Scientific Investigation in Greenland, 1951. 367p, 153p. (Reports on Greenland, vol. 152, nos. 1,2).
A collection of Eskimo legends, fables, myths, and fairy tales. Part one presents the actual texts with phonetics and transcription; part two provides a translation of the tales into English.

318 **Eskimo poems from Canada and Greenland.**
Translated by Tom Lowenstein. Pittsburgh, Pennsylvania: University of Pittsburgh Press; London: Allison & Busby, 1973. 152p.
An anthology of Eskimo poems and songs from Greenland and Canada, many never before translated into English. The poems deal with basic situations like hunting, fishing, dancing, lovemaking, and childbirth, and also include songs of mood, songs of derision, and charms. The translator provides extensive notes.

319 **Eskimo folk-tales.**
Collected by Knud Rasmussen, edited and translated from the Danish
by W. Worster. London, Copenhagen; Christiania, Norway:
Gyldendal, 1921. 156p.

A collection of stories and legends as told by Eskimo storytellers and transcribed by
the noted Danish explorer and student of Eskimo life. The tales, which are illustrated
by native Eskimo artists, have such titles as 'The woman who had a bear as a foster-
son', 'Imarasugssuaq, who ate his wives', and 'The giant dog'.

320 **Tales and traditions of the Eskimo.**
Henrik Rink. Montreal: McGill-Queen's University Press, 1974.
472p.

Rink became royal inspector or governor of South Greenland in 1858 and had much
opportunity for a close study of the Eskimos. He found their oral tradition a rich
source of information on social conditions and beliefs. Although the book provides
brief descriptions of Eskimo life, language, religion, society, customs, and laws, most
of it is comprised of folk tales. This is a reprint of the first edition (London,
Edinburgh; Blackwood and Sons, 1875) with a new introduction.

321 **The Greenlanders.**
Jane Smiley. New York: Alfred A. Knopf, 1988. 558p. maps.

In a harsh and forbidding yet beautiful land, a Viking colony struggles for survival. The
novel gives a vivid depiction of life in fourteenth century Greenland. Told in the style
of an old Norse saga, it portrays the bleakness of the settlers' lives and shows the
constant fears they experienced in a declining society.

N by E.
See item no. 229.

Eskimo life.
See item no. 236.

Juvenile fiction and non-fiction

322 **An Eskimo family.**
Bryan and Cherry Alexander. Minneapolis, Minnesota: Lerner
Publications, 1985. 31p. (Families Around the World).

Describes the life of a fifteen-year-old Eskimo boy and his family who live in the
world's most northern village, Siorapaluk, Greenland. Originally published as *Eskimo
boy* (London: A. & C. Black, 1979).

323 **Greenland: island at the top of the world.**
Madelyn Klein Anderson.   New York: Dodd, Mead, 1983. 127p.
maps. bibliog.
This book explains the geography and traces the history of Greenland for young readers.

324 **The great white.**
Jane and Paul Annixter.   New York: Holiday House, 1966. 159p.
The story of a battle for survival between Nunku, an Eskimo boy, and a huge polar bear, Iskwao (the great white). The book has been praised for the accuracy of its natural history. Intended for readers aged eleven to fifteen.

325 **Greenland in story and pictures.**
Bernadine Bailey.   Chicago: Albert Whitman, 1942. [n.p.] maps.
A 'pictured geography' of Greenland, for children.

326 **Eskimos.**
Mary Bringle.   New York: Franklin Watts, 1973. 87p. map. bibliog.
A survey for young readers of Eskimo life in Greenland and other Arctic areas, with descriptions of climate, animals, dwellings, clothing, families, hunting, food, customs and religious beliefs, entertainment, and art. Some attention is also given to recent changes in the traditional way of life and to problems and prospects for the Eskimo.

327 **Jon the unlucky.**
Elizabeth Coatsworth.   New York: Holt, Rinehart and Winston, 1964. 94p.
A tale of a young Danish boy who is orphaned in Greenland and seeks to support himself as a trapper, hunter, and fisher. He finds a hidden valley where descendants of Viking settlers are living secretly. For ages ten to twelve.

328 **Eskimos of the world.**
Paul Michael Elliott.   New York: Julian Messner, 1976. 128p.
This book presents the young reader with a brief history of the Eskimos and their past and present ways of life, and discusses the problems they face in adapting to the modern culture surrounding them.

329 **Whaling boy.**
Peter Freuchen.   New York: Putnam, 1958. 127p.
The adventures of a twelve-year-old boy on a Danish whaling ship.

330 **Eskimo boy.**
Pipaluk Freuchen.   Boston, Massachusetts: Lothrop, Lee & Shepard, 1951. 96p.
The story of a Greenland Eskimo boy who had to become the provider for his family after a walrus killed his father. The author is the daughter of Peter Freuchen, the Arctic explorer.

331 **To Greenland's icy mountains: the story of Hans Egede, explorer, colonist, missionary.**
Eve Garnett.   London: Heinemann, 1968. 190p. maps.
A biography, intended for young readers, of the Danish missionary who led the resettlement of Greenland in the eighteenth century.

332 **Leif the unlucky.**
Erik Christian Haugaard.   Boston, Massachusetts: Houghton Mifflin, 1982. 206p. map.
As the winters become increasingly harsh and the morale of the community deteriorates, a young man tries to rally the last few remaining colonists in fifteenth century Greenland.

333 **Eskimos.**
Wally Herbert.   Glasgow: Collins; New York: Franklin Watts, 1976. 128p. maps. bibliog.
The author, an Arctic and Antarctic explorer, lived among the Eskimos of northwest Greenland for two years. In this volume he provides a comprehensive introduction to Eskimo life for the mid-teens reader, explaining prehistory, mythology, the family, hunting, clothing, travel, and relations with the outside world, both past and present.

334 **Tobias catches trout.**
Ole Hertz, translated from the Danish by Tobi Tobias.   Minneapolis, Minnesota: Carolrhoda Books, 1984. 32p.
A young Greenlander goes fishing for trout with his family in their motor boat.

335 **Tobias goes ice fishing.**
Ole Hertz, translated from the Danish by Tobi Tobias.   Minneapolis, Minnesota: Carolrhoda Books, 1984. 32p.
A boy and his father fish through the ice that covers a Greenland fjord.

336 **Tobias goes seal hunting.**
Ole Hertz, translated from the Danish by Tobi Tobias.   Minneapolis, Minnesota: Carolrhoda Books, 1984. 32p.
A Greenland boy and his father hunt seals in their kayaks.

337 **Tobias has a birthday.**
Ole Hertz, translated from the Danish by Tobi Tobias.   Minneapolis, Minnesota: Carolrhoda Books, 1984. 32p.
Tobias, who lives in a Greenland village, celebrates his twelfth birthday in the traditional way with his family.

Literature. Juvenile fiction and non-fiction

338 Eskimos.
Jill Hughes. New York: Gloucester Press, 1978. 32p. map.

An introduction to the Eskimos and their world for children. Covers the Arctic seasons, birds and animals, igloos, clothing, travel, food, whaling, games and dances, and children's activities.

339 A family in Greenland.
Peter Otto Jacobsen, Preben Sejer Kristensen. New York: Bookwright Press, 1986. 32p. maps. (Families Around the World).

Description of the life of a family in a Greenland village.

340 Arctic exploration.
Douglas Liversidge. New York: Franklin Watts, 1970. 88p.

A history for young readers of the expeditions that, in the author's view, made the greatest contributions towards the exploration of the Arctic. Included are the Viking voyages to Greenland, the whale hunts of William Scoresby, and the establishment of the American scientific base at Camp Century.

341 Two against the Arctic: the story of a restless life between Greenland and Alaska.
Kurt Lutgen, translated from the German by Isabel and Florence McHugh. New York: Pantheon, 1957. 239p. maps.

An adventure story of two men's conflict with Arctic hazards in Greenland and Alaska, based upon actual fact. The book received a prize as the best book for young readers published in Germany in 1955.

342 Fridtjof Nansen: Arctic explorer.
Francis Edward Noel-Baker. New York: Putnam, 1958. 126p.

The life of the famous Arctic explorer and scientist who led several arduous Greenland expeditions. Intended for readers aged twelve to fourteen.

343 Iceland and Greenland.
Helen E. Peck. London; New York; Toronto: Abelard-Schuman, 1966. 125p. maps.

Approximately half of this book provides an introduction to Greenland for readers of ten to fourteen years of age. Included is basic information on geography, the people and their life styles, history, economics, and culture.

344 Hans, the Eskimo: his story of Arctic adventures with Kane, Hayes, and Hall.
Edwin Gile Rich. Boston, Massachusetts: Houghton Mifflin, 1934. 288p.

The story of three famous polar expeditions – those of Kane in 1853, Hayes in 1860, and the Polaris in 1871 – told in the first person as if by Hans Christian, a South Greenland Eskimo who accompanied them. Based on the narratives of the three expeditions and related for the young reader.

Art, Music and Theatre

345 Eskimo art.
   Cottie Burland.   London: Hamlyn, 1973. 96p. map. bibliog.
An illustrated history of Eskimo art, including that of Greenland, from prehistoric
times to the present.

346 Dance masks of Ammassalik (east coast of Greenland).
   Robert Gessain.   *Arctic Anthropology*, vol. 21, no. 2 (1984), p. 81-
   107.
The Ammassalimiut of East Greenland carved human face masks from driftwood to
wear for drum dancing. This article discusses the history of the masks, the details of
their manufacture, and the carvers who made them. Fifty-two photographs of masks
are included.

347 The Tukaq theatre: a cultural 'harpoon head'.
   Kirsten Thonsgaard Hansen.   *Arctic Anthropology*, vol. 23, nos. 1-2
   (1986), p. 347-57. bibliog.
An account of the first tour of Greenland, in 1978, by the first professional
Greenlandic theatre. Analyses the play 'Inuit' performed on that tour and the
Greenlandic audiences' reactions to it.

348 Traditional and acculturated Greenlandic music.
   Michael Hauser.   *Arctic Anthropology*, vol. 23, nos. 1-2 (1986),
   p. 359-86.
Traditional music is disappearing in Greenland, but in the southernmost and
northernmost areas, interesting relics of traditional music and some adapted whalers'
dances remain. Fifteen songs and an instrumental dance are reviewed.

Art, Music and Theatre

349 **Classification of traditional Greenland music.**
Michael Hauser, H. C. Petersen. Copenhagen: Commission for
Scientific Research, 1985. 50p. bibliog.
A general survey of Greenlandic music, concentrating on traditional forms but
including a section on European and American influences. This appeared in the
periodical *Meddelelser om Grønland: Man and Society* no. 7.

350 **The art of Greenland: sculpture, crafts, painting.**
Bodil Kaalund, translated from the Danish by Kenneth Tindall.
Berkeley and Los Angeles, California; London: University of
California Press, 1983. 224p. bibliog.
A comprehensive description of the art of Greenland from earliest times to the
present. The author, herself a painter and a co-founder of the Art School of
Greenland, defines art broadly so as to include clothing and implements as well as
sculpture and painting; and she accompanies her history and criticism with numerous
illustrations in colour and black-and-white.

351 **Motifs behind the masks.**
Bodil Kaalund. *Scandinavian Review*, vol. 69, no. 3 (Sept. 1981),
p. 6-17.
On the myths, magic and mysteries behind the masks of Greenland, a traditional art
form.

352 **New currents in Greenlandic music: from traditional to contemporary
music.**
Birgit Lynge. *Arctic Anthropology*, vol. 23, nos. 1-2 (1986), p. 387-99.
bibliog.
A description of the diverse forms of contemporary music. Recent Greenlandic music
has a special sound that reflects both traditional music and modern influences.

353 **Eskimo sculpture.**
Jørgen Meldgaard. London: Methuen, 1959. 48p. bibliog.
An illustrated discussion of Eskimo sculpture from Greenland and Canada, from
prehistoric times to the twentieth century. The author, a Danish archaeologist, is a
specialist in Eskimo studies.

Greenland: past and present.
See item no. 14.

The Eskimos.
See item no. 218.

Eskimo life.
See item no. 236.

Eskimos.
See item no. 326.

Aron from Kangeq and the Dano-Greenlandic museum cooperation.
See item no. 358.

Arctic.
See item no. 364.

Libraries and Museums

354 **Greenland's museum laws: an introduction to Greenland's museums under Home Rule.**
Claus Andreasen. *Arctic Anthropology*, vol. 23, nos. 1-2 (1986), p. 239-46. maps.
In 1981 Greenland took over from Denmark jurisdiction over its museums and antiquities. The article discusses the work of the Greenlandic National Museum and summarizes the content of the Museum Law and the functions of the Museum Council.

355 **Libraries in Scandinavia.**
K. C. Harrison. London: André Deutsch, 1969. 2nd rev. ed. 288p. bibliog.
Contains a very brief description (p. 81-82) of the development of public libraries in Greenland and their status in the 1960s.

356 **Polar and cold regions library resources: a directory.**
Edited by Robin Minion, Geraldine A. Cooke. Edmonton, Alberta: Northern Libraries Colloquy, University of Alberta, Institute for Northern Studies. 2nd ed. 383p.
A directory of 162 libraries, archives, and collections dealing with the polar regions, representing twenty-two countries. Included from Greenland is information on the holdings and policies of the Geological Survey of Greenland Library, the National Library of Greenland, and the Arctic Station Library.

357 **The public library legislation of the Nordic countries: Greenland.**
Scandinavian Public Library Quarterly, vol.19, no. 5 (1986), p. 157-59.
The texts of the Library Act for Greenland, November 29, 1978, and the Landsting's Ordinance No. 4 of 15 October 1979, on the library system.

358 **Aron from Kangeq and the Dano–Greenlandic museum cooperation.**
Emil Rosing, Birte Haagen. *Arctic Anthropology*, vol. 23, nos. 1-2
(1986), p. 247-58. bibliog.
Discusses the cooperative arrangements between the National Museums of Denmark and Greenland and the return of art and artifacts to Greenland. The watercolours of Aron from Kangeq and Jens Kreutzmann were the first to be returned.

359 **Public libraries in Denmark.**
Leif Thorsen, translated from the Danish by Mogens Kay- Larsen.
Copenhagen: Danish Institute (Det Danske Selskab), 1972. 176p.
A brief but comprehensive treatment of the libraries of Denmark, Greenland, and the Faroes. The book discusses library legislation, national and local government administration, finance, central libraries, library collections and activities, school and children's libraries, research libraries, the book trade and the authors, the training of librarians and Nordic and international co-operation. The work was reprinted with a supplement in 1975.

360 **Changes in the National Library of Greenland.**
Hans Westermann, Benny Høyer.   In: *Arctica 1978: 7th Northern Libraries Colloquy, 19-23 September 1978*. Edited by Sylvie Devers.
Paris: Éditions du Centre National de la Recherche Scientifique, 1982,
p. 273-77.
A history of the development of the National Library of Greenland and a description of its present facilities and collections.

Groenlandica. Catalogue of the Groenlandica-collection in the National Library of Greenland.
See item no. 368.

Newspapers and Periodicals

Greenlandic and Danish publications

361 **Atuagagdliutit/Grønlandsposten.** (Greenland's Post).
Godthåb/Nuuk, 1861- . weekly.
Greenland's national weekly and the oldest newspaper in Greenland. The text is in Danish and Greenlandic.

362 **Meddelelser om Grønland.** (Information about Greenland).
Copenhagen: Kommissionen for videnskabelige undersøgelser i Grønland, 1879- . irregular.
A journal published by the Commission for Scientific Research in Greenland, with frequent articles in English. Since 1979 it has been divided into three different series: *Bioscience, Geoscience, and Man and Society*.

363 **Sermitsiaq.**
Godthåb/Nuuk, weekly.
This weekly newspaper is widely read throughout Greenland.

Greenland: past and present.
See item no. 14.

The spread of printing – western hemisphere – Greenland.
See item no. 194.

Other publications

364 **Arctic.**
Calgary, Alberta: University of Calgary, Arctic Institute of North
America, 1948- . quarterly.

This covers all areas of Arctic scholarship (including education, engineering, fine arts,
humanities, medicine, science, and social science) dealing with the polar and subpolar
regions of the world.

365 **Arctic and Alpine Research.**
Boulder, Colorado: Institute of Arctic and Alpine Research, University
of Colorado, 1969- . quarterly.

A journal covering topics on all aspects of the high latitude and mountainous areas of
the world. Articles on Greenland are occasionally included.

366 **Arctic Anthropology.**
Madison, Wisconsin: University of Wisconsin Press, 1962- . biannual.

An international journal devoted to the study of the northern peoples and cultures,
past and present. Articles deal with archaeology, ethnology, ethnohistory, linguistics,
human biology, and related fields.

Bibliographies

367 **Greenland since 1979: an annotated, cross-referenced bibliography.**
Edited by France Benoit.   Ottawa: Circumpolar and Scientific Affairs
Directorate, Department of Indian Affairs and Northern
Development,1989. 292p.
A bibliography of recent works on Greenland, with references in English, French,
Danish, and Greenlandic.

368 **Groenlandica. Catalogue of the Groenlandica-collection in the National
Library of Greenland.**
Edited by Benny Høyer.   Nuuk/Godthåb: Nunatta Atuagaateqarfia,
1986. 585p.
This catalogue of the holdings on Greenland in the island's National Library includes
books in Greenlandic, books about Greenland and the Arctic regions, and several
indexes. There are brief notes on each of the books.

369 **Physical anthropology in Greenland.**
J. Balslev Jørgensen.   In: *Arctica 1978: 7th Northern Libraries
Colloquy, 19-23 September 1978.* Edited by Sylvie Devers. Paris:
Éditions du Centre National de la Recherche Scientifique, 1982, p. 193.
A very brief listing of volumes that have extensive bibliographies on physical
anthropology in Greenland.

370 **The Arctic.**
H. G. R. King.   Oxford; Santa Barbara, California; Denver,
Colorado: Clio Press, 1989. 272p. map. (World Bibliographical Series,
vol. 99).
A select, annotated bibliography of 935 books, journal articles, conference proceedings, and theses, covering a wide range of subjects dealing with the Arctic and sub-Arctic regions, including Greenland.

371 **The Indians and Eskimos of North America: a bibliography of books in print through 1972.**
Jack W. Marken.   Vermillion, South Dakota: Dakota Press,
University of South Dakota, 1973. 200p.
This is primarily a bibliography on North American Indians but lists a number of books on the Greenland Eskimos. The volume's usefulness, however, is weakened by its lack of an index.

372 **Denmark.**
Kenneth E. Miller.   Oxford; Santa Barbara, California; Denver,
Colorado: Clio Press, 1987. 216p. map. (World Bibliographical Series,
vol. 83).
Includes a brief annotated bibliography of basic works on Greenland.

373 **Ethnographic bibliography of North America.**
George Peter Murdock.   New Haven, Connecticut: Human Relations
Area Files, 1960. 3rd ed. 393p. maps.
A bibliography of books and articles on tribal groups in North America, including works on the East Greenland Eskimos (p. 12-15), the Polar Eskimos (p. 23-24), and the West Greenland Eskimos (p. 30-33).

374 **Scandinavia: a bibliographic survey of literature.**
United States Department of the Army.   Washington, DC:
Government Printing Office, 1975. 121p. maps.
Annotated bibliography on the military, political, economic and sociological aspects of Scandinavia, with chapters on the region as a whole as well as on Denmark (including Greenland and the Faroes) and the other individual countries. The selections are quite limited in number and drawn mainly from periodicals.

375 **Arctic bibliography.**
Edited by Marie Tremaine et al.   Washington, DC: Department of
Defense; Montreal; London: McGill-Queen's University Press,
1953-75. 16 vols. maps.
An exhaustive and well-indexed bibliography of books and papers on the Arctic, drawn from publications in forty languages. Each citation has an abstract in English. There are many listings for Greenland, under such sub-headings as administration and government, archaeology, birds, botany, construction, economic and social conditions, education, fisheries, glaciers, inland ice, laws, maps, meteorology, mineral resources,

palaeontology, public health, and zoology. The series ended in 1975 when no more funds were available for the project.

Icebergs: a bibliography relevant to eastern Canadian waters.
See item no. 129.

Bibliography on Greenlandic botany.
See item no. 143.

Swimmers and sea birds.
See item no. 155.

Arctic archaeology: a bibliography and history.
See item no. 169.

Bibliography of bibliographies on the Inuit.
See item no. 232.

Alaska native languages: a bibliographical catalogue. Part one: Indian languages.
See item no. 248.

Greenland medical bibliography.
See item no. 268.

Past and contemporary administrative problems in Greenland.
See item no. 280.

Index

The index is a single alphabetical sequence of authors and translators, titles of publications and subjects. Index entries refer both to the main items and to other works mentioned in the notes to each item. Title entries are in italics. Numbers refer to bibliographic entries. For indexing purposes, the Danish letters å, æ, and ø have been treated as corresponding to the letters a, ae, and o.

Map of Greenland

This map shows the more important towns and other features.

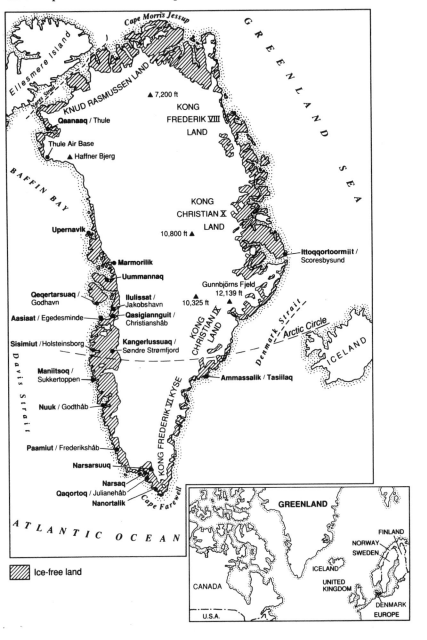

Ice-free land